Sister
to Sister

Sister to Sister

Devotions

for and from
African American Women

Suzan D. Johnson Cook, Editor

Judson Press ® Valley Forge

Sister to Sister: Devotions for and from African
American Women
© 1995 Judson Press, Valley Forge, PA 19482-0851

Unless otherwise noted, Bible quotations in this volume are
from *The Holy Bible,* King James Version.

Other quotations are from the New Revised Standard Version
of the Bible, copyrighted 1989 by the Division of Christian Educa-
tion of the National Council of the Churches of Christ in the USA.
Used by permission. All rights reserved. Revised Standard Version
of the Bible, copyright © 1946, 1952, 1971, by the Division of
Christian Education of the National Council of the Churches of
Christ in the USA. Used by permission. HOLY BIBLE: *New
International Version,* copyright © 1973, 1978, 1984. Used by
permission of Zondervan Bible Publishers. The New King James
Version. Copyright © 1972, 1984 by Thomas Nelson Inc.

Copyright for "A Woman's Place" (p. 187) is held by Rev.
Martha Simmons. Permissions requests should be directed to Rev.
Simmons.

Library of Congress Cataloging-in-Publication Data
    Sister to sister : devotions for and from African American
women / Suzan D. Johnson Cook, editor.
        p. cm.
      ISBN 0-8170-1221-4 (pbk. : alk. paper)
        1. Afro-American women—Prayer-books and devotions—
English. I. Johnson Cook, Suzan D. (Suzan Denise), 1957-   .
      BV4844.S545 1995
      242'.643'08996073—dc20 95-19350

Printed in the U.S.A.
07 06 05 04 03 02 01 00
15 14 13 12 11 10

In loving memory of

My grandmother,
Leona Fisher Starnes Thomas

My favorite aunts,
Martha Springs Porcher and
Katherine Hayes Cyrus

And in honor of

My mother, Dorothy C. Johnson

My niece, Jessica Ashley Johnson

The women of Rendall Memorial
Presbyterian Church

The women of P.S. 194 in Manhattan

And all the women in my life who have
loved me and cared

Contents

Introduction

What a blessing it has been to compile this book of meditations for and from my sisters!

I have had the honor and privilege of working with and knowing some powerful, beautiful, spirit-filled, soulful African American women. Maya Angelou, in one of her poems, calls us "phenomenal," and I must agree. Something wonderful is happening around the nation and around the globe as sisters are beginning to care for and be concerned about one another with a remarkable vigor and renewed vitality and commitment I have not witnessed since my teenage years.

As I was growing up, I was tall and athletic in days when sports were not as encouraged or as popular for women as they are today. In those days I gravitated towards males and joined them in stickball, punchball, basketball, and other games known to us inner-city kids who played on the streets after school. I built igloos in the snow with my brother and his friends, rode bikes to the shopping malls and beaches, and had snowball fights. Sometimes I played with dolls and jumped rope. It was a very healthy childhood.

But that was during the school year.

In the summers, especially in my elementary and junior high school days, our parents would send us South to the "women of Melrose Place" (they actually lived on a street called Melrose Drive, in Concord, North Carolina)—to my grandmother "Mama" and Aunt Bee, who would help me to "be a lady." It was part of the refining process and the unofficial rite of passage experienced by many of my northern playmates and me. We were fortunate to have relatives in the South. The instruction was to help us be well-rounded, balanced human beings, but most importantly, women. They prepared wonderful soul-food meals of red-eyed gravy, ham, biscuits, and grits which they hoped I would be able to re-create on my own as they tried to teach me how to bake, cook, sew, can preserves, and crochet, although most of the time I preferred to play softball and run in the red clay fields. But they cared for me. They listened to me. They loved me. They took me around from house to house, introducing me to and familiarizing me with my family members—cousins and aunts and uncles—who always prepared my favorite foods and received their updates from "up North" from me. They spent numerous hours preparing me for and coaching me through this thing called life. They were the primary women, along with my Aunt Katherine in Washington, who "spoiled" me and to whom I could speak at any hour of the night, even into my college years and adulthood. I could trust and confide in them. I gladly received discipline from them. They were my first friends, and I am grateful that I had them in my life. We loved each other, and they taught me how to pray and know God for myself. They affirmed me as an African American woman and encouraged me to not only reach for my dreams but to exceed them.

I remember so well my eighth-grade year in a predominantly white prep school when I wanted to wear my hair in an "Afro" and the girls teased me. Mama told me to go and "paint that school black." In her own way she was telling me not to compromise who I was and not to give in to the majority culture. Not only did I continue to wear my hair in the styles I preferred, but I went on to be the first black president of the junior school. Mama smiled with me.

Katherine, Bee, and Mama were able to live to see my graduation day from college, and although I had only four tickets for family, they came, along with three carloads of my relatives. It was as if they were saying, "We had a part in your development as a woman, and we will be there to see you 'cross over.' " They now have crossed over to the other side. I miss them, but a part of each of them is in me.

It was these women, along with my mother, Dorothy, and her wonderful friends, mostly women who taught at P. S. 194 in Harlem in the 60s and 70s—teachers who cared compassionately about their students and their families— who introduced me to the other heroes and "sheroes" of our heritage. They taught me that "becoming a lady," specifically an African American woman in this society, would require knowing more than childhood games; it would necessitate knowing about and fortifying myself for life's games, encompassed in racism, sexism, and classism, and still being able to have strong morals and character in spite of it all.

Church was also important. We worshiped with the leadership of the emerging black middle class, who were all very proud, capable, and determined to "be somebody," not only for themselves, but also for those of us who were watching and emulating them. My father and mother were in that group and were starting our family business at that time, which today still thrives in its thirty-third year of operation.

So I had women and men in my life as mentors, role models, and family members who taught me how to survive. But I learned something special, something different, from the women in my life, and it wasn't until I compiled this book that I stopped to reflect on and appreciate those learnings.

Sister to Sister: Devotions for and from African American Women is a book that I hope will move, motivate, mature, mold, transform, teach, heal, breathe, open up wounds, heal wounds, restore, resuscitate. It is a collection of reflections that I think every African American woman should have not only in her library but also in her pocket or pocketbook. It was in the receiving and reading of these meditations that I saw how ministering to one another can go far beyond a pulpit or parish setting. Healing came for two of my sister-friends as they were able for the first time in years to share their stories of grief over the deaths of their sons, one who died as a child after leading his mom to Christ, the other in the height of his college years. Both are women of whom I have been very fond for years. I knew of their pain but could never ask them, nor could they tell, what happened. But something happened in the evolution of this book: they and others like them were set free. Perhaps you will connect with some of the stories in this book and find your moments of release as well.

Sister to Sister contains stories of mothers and daughters, and sometimes both have contributed to the book. You will encounter meditations of love, of loss, of failure, of success. All ages have contributed. Some are friends I've known for years, some are friends of friends, still others are friends' mothers and aunts; some are sister ministers, some are daughters in ministry. From each we have something to learn, to affirm, to appreciate, to deny, to reclaim, to ask, to answer.

Sister to Sister is about us—women—in our wholeness and recovering from our brokenness. We are teachers, doctors, daughters, mothers, aunts, grandmothers, granddaughters, lawyers, ministers, artists, dancers—women who, although we may not know each other individually and personally, have created what I call "sister-strength," which is the collective strength and responsibility we have to and for one another. We have become the modern-day balm to and for one another. Although I no longer physically have with me the "women of Melrose Place," I have these new sisters and, thank God, I still have my mother, with whom I developed a new relationship as I became a wife and mother. Suddenly, her little girl is now a mother herself. Now I am an aunt of Jessica and her brother, Charles, and I can't help but wonder how I can provide nurturing for them as my aunts did for me.

Many call me a woman of God, although that is what I am trying to attain. I am now part of a predominantly male profession, which is slowly reforming itself as the twenty-first century approaches. As a wife and mother, I think of the image of a woman described in Proverbs 31. I hope that my children—a two-year-old, Samuel David, and one born during the compiling of this book, Christopher Daniel—will rise up and call me blessed and that my husband will see me as a virtuous woman who tries to keep happiness in our home and our relationship.

I am still an athletic woman. My moves have changed, and I've slowed down quite a bit. I enjoy watching the younger women, especially those talented and disciplined enough to make the Olympics. I now *watch* more than I *play* as a new generation of inner-city kids have traded punchball and softball for other games. I am woman—unashamedly and unapologetically. I am minister, wife, mother, pastor, friend, sister, daughter, and aunt. And I have been blessed in order to bless others. I hope this book will be a blessing to those who read it. It sure has been to me!

Linda M. Aina

Women on the Move

"Call unto me, and I will answer thee, and shew thee great and mighty things, which thou knowest not." —*Jeremiah 33:3*

Looking back over the past twenty years of my life, I can say that I have traveled far and wide. My journeys have taken me from the jungles of Venezuela to the hilly streets of San Francisco and from the markets of Lagos, Nigeria, to the Inner Harbor of Baltimore, Maryland. I have been blessed with safe sojourn and benefits along the way—multicultural experiences, lasting friendships, and opportunities to share and grow. But most importantly, I have been on a faith journey in which I have learned, with each new road traveled, to put my faith and trust in God.

African American women have always been on the move. Our foremothers endured the long, hard journey from their African homeland; they migrated from the rural South to seek a better life in the North; and today's mobile black woman travels locally and globally, making community and corporate connections.

We cannot stand still if we expect to grow. In our quest for new opportunities, career advancement, and fulfilling personal goals, we are often required to travel a distance. It may mean relocating, separating from family and friends, and leaving those things that are familiar. But by taking the faith journey, we open ourselves to God's guidance and direction.

Give God ultimate control; surrender your will to God's will. When you get on the road with faith and operate with the assurance that God will see you safely through, new pathways will open; even the roadblocks experienced will be temporary. Go with God and, as you journey, reflect on God's grace, pray without ceasing, and frequently consult God's road map, the Word. I have discovered that, no matter where I go or how far I travel, God is always there. God stands ready to empower, uplift, and guide us in our faith journeys.

Thought for the Day: In all your ways acknowledge God, and God will direct your paths (see Proverbs 3:6).

Linda M. Aina is a vice-president of the United Way of Bridgeport, Connecticut. A native of New York, she is a B.A. graduate of Fisk University in Nashville, Tennessee, and earned a master's in public administration. She was awarded an ITT fellowship to study in Caracas, Venezuela. Extremely active in the church and propelled by her Christian faith, she also works with ACTSO, a youth leadership development program of the NAACP.

Natalie P. Alford

Divine Counselor

> *"He has sent Me to heal the broken-hearted." —Luke 4:18b (NKJV)*

Inevitably each of us will suffer from a broken heart. When this happens, prepared or not, we will be caught in a life experience that we can't escape. When this happens, it will be necessary for us to draw strength from loved ones and from the Spirit of God.

My mother died on August 26, 1986, but sometimes it feels like yesterday. We had a special relationship that I believe began with my nine-month gestation period. During that time, I was veiled in the unseen, the unexpressed, and the unarticulated. Mama called me—the only child born to this union—her "one young 'un." I remember doing the fun things in life with her—

shopping, amusement parks, movies, traveling, cookouts, or just sitting around the house talking with relatives and friends. I loved my mother dearly, and as the years passed, I learned to love her even more.

Several days after her physical, the news came that my mother had lung cancer. My breath seemed to exit my body. At the sound of the words "lung cancer," I cried, "My God!" The surgeon removed one lung, and Mama and I enjoyed the next five years together. Then the call came from my daddy. God had called my mom to her resting place.

I was faced with a severed mother-daughter relationship—and a broken heart. An emotional reaction was set into motion, and it hurt. It hurt in the morning. It hurt in the middle of the day. It hurt during the night. That special place in my heart was pierced with a deep void that I felt could never be filled. There I was, all alone in Orlando, sipping from the bitter cup of grief. This permanency and totality of separation produced an intense, overwhelming sadness.

The ache was beyond description, and those who had never experienced such brokenhearted-ness could provide no solace. Some friends and loved ones thought I should hurry up, get over it, and go on with my life as if nothing significant had happened. When someone told me, "At least she's not suffering anymore," I wondered why she had to suffer at all. Someone else said that I'd feel better soon—but this was no cold or upset stomach I needed to get over! My experience was personal, unique, sacred. I needed time.

When no one else could provide comfort, my greatest adviser was the Divine Counselor. I held on to the promise that the power for mending broken hearts belongs only to the One for whom all things are possible. I remembered that when I have no one else, I always have Jesus. With God's help, I learned to smile again. Thank you, God, for being patient with me.

Thought for the Day: God has smiled on me, and today I smile again.

Rev. Natalie P. Alford, M.Div., is the program manager for the National Resource Center for the Development of Ethical Leadership from the Black Church Tradition at the Colgate Rochester Divinity School, Rochester, New York. Formerly a corporate executive administrator, she is an ordained itinerant elder in the African Methodist Episcopal church and a doctoral student at the University of Rochester.

Jetola E. Anderson

Presumed Incompetent

In our society African American women must face the presumption of incompetence every day. It doesn't matter what credentials we bring to the table——degrees, experience, letters of recommendation, and so on; there is little or no exemption from the presumption. We live with the insulting notion that we are a mistake or a quota project of sorts. We are presumed incompetent until we walk on water, and then we hear it's because we don't know how to swim or we are too intimidating or aggressive. In the meantime, others are presumed competent until they show otherwise, and then they have the luxury of forgiveness.

Nathan McCall and Marvin Gaye are not the only ones who want to holler. Black women all over America want to holler because we are so sick and tired of being fourth-class citizens. It's a slap in the face when a black woman wearing a suit gets on an airplane and is automatically assumed to be a flight attendant. It hurts when a full-time professional/part-time grad student is asked "What team are you on?" because the unspoken accusation is "You couldn't possible be here on academic or financial merit, so you must be on an athletic scholarship."

Faced with these subtle and sometimes blatant messages every day, it would be easy for us to internalize them and even believe them. However, we cannot afford to make that mistake. We must combat the negative messages every step of the way. We are proud people from proud stock based on a supreme design by the Creator. Harriet Tubman and Madame C. J. Walker would weep in their graves if we gave up our rightful place or ran away from the fight.

We have to feed our minds and spirits with positive and nutritious thoughts. We must surround ourselves with positive people who believe in themselves and in us and will constantly encourage us to keep on reaching for higher heights. We must read positive, self-affirming books and poetry (personally, I love Maya Angelou's poem "Phenomenal Woman"), and we must listen to good, soul-healing music. Additionally, we must treat ourselves well in every regard, especially physically. Every day we go off to war—and we have to put on our full armor.

Above all, we must always remember that we were created in the image of greatness and can do all things through Christ who strengthens us (see Philippians 4:13). No matter how others try to keep us down, if we refuse to give in, we will keep on rising.

> My Creator, my Maker, I thank you for designing me for a special purpose. I know that you have given me the tools and the competence to fulfill that purpose. Lord, help me not to be distracted or derailed from that purpose. Help me to keep my vision focused on your greater plan. I accept your love and your grace today and every day. Amen.

Thought for the Day: "I press toward the mark for the prize of the high calling of God in Christ Jesus" (Philippians 3:14).

Jetola E. Anderson is a human resources representative for ARCO Chemical in Houston, Texas. She earned her B.A. in psychology and Spanish from SUNY (State University of New York) Plattsburgh, her M.B.A. in management from Villanova University, and was featured in the 1991 New York edition of *Success Guide* as one of "Ten to Watch."

Coral C. Aubert

A Mother and Her Sons

The Lord has blessed me with two sons whom I love dearly. I never thought much about mother-son relations because I always felt duty-bound when it came to them. When they were growing up, I thought more about their father-son relationship; African American boys need a male image in their lives.

My husband and I always ardently wanted children—on the condition that we be financially ready. But as God would have it, my first son was neither conceived nor born at the most opportune time in our marriage. Nevertheless, his birth was a miracle in my life. The birth of my second son seventeen months later was the next miracle. Their impact on my life was awesome. Besides loving them, I was in a constant state of anxiety and disbelief, however. I use the word *disbelief* because at that time I could not imagine anything of that magnitude happening to me. I hadn't accepted Jesus Christ as my personal Lord and Savior yet. I believed in God, but I was still playing at my faith and at church.

While my sons were growing up, I remember pleading with God to grant me enough time on this earth to see my sons grow to manhood. I also recited to him that I believed that it was more important for me to love them than for them to love me. I wanted to love them like God loved his Son. Invoking this belief as a parent often translates into taking some tough, unpopular stands and making some tough, unpopular decisions.

The Lord fulfilled my wish; I've seen my sons grow to manhood, and they are both wonderful young men full of love, giving, and talent. In addition, I accepted Jesus Christ as my personal Lord and Savior five years ago, after undergoing a major life-threatening illness and surgery. During that time when they thought that I might not make it, my sons showed the depth of their love for me. Praise the Lord! They still continue today showing that concern.

I thank the Lord every day for my sons, and I pray every day that they will come to know Jesus Christ as their Lord and Savior. They've seen the wonderful things that the Lord has done in the past five years. They've seen the joy the Lord has given me. They've seen the peace. They've heard me give thanks and praise to God unashamedly. They've witnessed me openly praying and reading the Bible. King Hezekiah expresses it beautifully in Isaiah 38:18-19: "For the grave cannot praise thee, death cannot celebrate thee: they that go down into the pit cannot hope for thy truth. The living, the living, he shall praise thee, as I do this day: the father to the children shall make known thy truth."

Prayer and devotion were not common practices in our home when my sons were growing up. Yes, they went to church. Yes, they knew and understood that there was a God, but they didn't know him as "my God"; they didn't know him personally. You see, I used to think that my husband and I were calling most of the shots in our sons' lives. I believed that as long as we lived the so-called good life, daily family devotions and prayer were not necessary. Since coming to know Jesus, trying to walk the Christian walk, and trying to become better acquainted with the Holy Spirit, I can now see how truly blind and ignorant I was. I pray every day that it's not too late and that I'll see my sons accept Jesus as their personal Lord and Savior. I see signs of the Lord working on that request.

Thought for the Day: God is love. On this day express love to as many as you can and receive love from as many who are willing to share it, for love is the greatest gift (see 1 Corinthians 13).

Coral C. Aubert, an executive in the banking industry for several years, is now a financial/business consultant. She serves on the cabinet of the Mariners' Temple Baptist Church in New York City, where she holds the office of church treasurer and is involved in the lives of children who grew up in "welfare hotels."

Bernita W. Babb

If Pillows Could Talk

According to the dictionary, a "pillow" is a case of cloth stuffed with some yielding material, or inflated with air, used as a support for the head, as in sleeping. A "pillar" is a firm, upright, separate support, as a column or shaft or monument that supports a work or cause. Both terms, *pillow* and *pillar,* are found in the Bible.

If pillows could talk, what stories they would tell of inner thoughts and feelings, of dreams and celestial visitations, had by those whose heads they gently hold and support. They would speak lowly, mediocre, and wondrous words of joy and happiness experienced, of confidences disclosed, burdens shared, and tears absorbed. If only pillows could talk, they would comfort, console, correct, confirm, counsel, congratulate, confide, warn, and prophesy!

If pillows could talk, they would tell of ancient times when Jesus was asleep on a pillow in the stern of the ship and his disciples despaired. They would tell how Jesus arose, rebuked the wind, and calmed the raging sea, saying, "Peace, be still!" They would tell of how Jacob came to Bethel and tarried there all night, how he took the stones of that place and used them for a pillow and laid down to sleep, how he dreamed about a ladder on which the angels of God ascended and descended from earth to heaven. If pillows could talk, they would echo Ezekiel's prophetic warning: "Woe to the women that sew pillows for every elbow to rest upon, and make covering for the head of every age to lead them astray, to hunt the souls of men who will consult them about their problems. Will you promise your victims life?" (Ezekiel 13:18, paraphrased).

My pillow knows that, as prophetess, I am not guilty of leading others astray, of pretending to give revelations and guidance, or of hunting the souls of others who consult about their problems.

Indeed, if my pillow could talk, it would tell of my seven-year quest for the simple privilege of performing the selfless vocation to which God has called and anointed me. It would concede that no one should have to struggle so hard to be

15

given the right to be a blessing. It would tell of the tears it absorbed as, by faith, I persevered.

My pillow knows that if I had to do it all again, I would. I could. It is reconciled to the fact that becoming a female pastor means breaking down barriers, forming new paradigms, and knowing that God in Christ Jesus will set us free. It means knowing that God in Christ Jesus can use anybody to do God's will. It means knowing that on Easter morning Christ arose—and now all who believe will also be set free and given treasures and gifts in our earthly vessels to be used for the glory of God.

I am encouraged by the silence of my pillow, for just as Jacob set up his pillow as a pillar (or monument) of his encounter with the angels, I set up my pillow also as pillar or monument to persevere by and through the grace of God.

Thought for the Day: Hallelujah! We'll understand it better by and by.

Rev. Bernita W. Babb, who lives in the Bronx, is a pastor in the Reformed Church in America and an associate for congregational ministries. She is the first African American woman to receive a pastorate in the Reformed Church of America.

Marjorie A. Boston

The Value of Pain

On December 25, 1967, I gave birth to a wonderful baby boy whom we named Scott. For the eleven years of his life, he was a joy and a spiritual blessing. My husband, Scott, and I were a happy family, sharing what I thought to be the fullness of life. We had vacations, school activities, and great family gatherings. But although our family was happy, there was a void, for we had not placed God in the center of our joy.

During a personal struggle, when I felt as if I had no place to turn, my son, then seven, told me, "You need to go to church and get saved," assuring me that I would feel better. I took his words to heart and allowed him to take me to the church of his choice. As the pastor gave the invitation to discipleship, my son yelled, "Get up and join the church, Ma! You ain't got no church!" Although embarrassed and nervous, I immediately moved from my seat into the aisle and proceeded to join the church.

While walking home, my son, bubbling with excitement, looked up and said, "I'm really glad you joined this church, Ma, 'cause you're gonna need this church one day." The following Sunday, Scott also joined the church and shortly thereafter, we were baptized. Life had a new radiance, for Jesus was now the center of our joy.

Four years later, on a beautiful fall Sunday after Sunday school and the church service, Scott went for a bicycle ride—and abruptly our joy was dismantled. Our son, our only child, was fatally struck by a reckless driver. During the time Scott was in a coma, I maintained a strength that was without a doubt my help from the Lord for, needless to say, the pain was excruciating. It was the greatest agony I've ever had to endure. The suffering was so intense that I felt I would not be able to function again. With my face and spirit hanging down to the ground, I remember saying, "Where do I go from here? What's going to happen? What are my husband and I to do?"

I found strength in the Holy Scriptures and the profound quote of Kahlil Gibran in *The Prophet* (New York: Alfred A. Knopf, 1968): "Your children are not your children. They are the sons and daughters of life, longing for itself. They come through you but not from you, and though they are with you, yet they belong not to you." After six weeks in a coma, Scott died. But through faith, hope, and God's grace and mercy, I was kept whole and ultimately able to bring solace to our family and friends.

During this time, I came to understand the prophetic words of my son: "You will need this church some day." For if it had not been for the Lord on my side, our pastor, and our church community, I would not have survived. I thank God for giving me the blessing of a child that led me to the Word of God. I have learned that pain has value when you invite God into your tragedies as well as your joys.

Yes, my son, my leader, has gone to be with the Lord. However, his valuable gift of leading me to Jesus Christ and to the power of the Holy Spirit has empowered me to rise up from my infirmity and take up the challenge to respond to the call. Yes, it brings healing to the pain.

Thought for the Day: If it had not been for the Lord on my side, where would I be? Let Jesus be the center of your joy!

Rev. Marjorie A. Boston is the coordinator and developer of the prison outreach ministries of Grace Baptist Church in Mount Vernon, New York.

Audrey F. Bronson

The Strength Is in the Struggle

Black women have been and continue to be a major strength in the African American community. With more than half our families headed by and supported by women, we have had to endure many, many struggles. Black women struggle under the triple jeopardy of racism, sexism, and classism more than any other segment of our society. In spite of this—this truth struck me like a bolt of lightening out of the blue—very seldom do black women commit suicide. People commit suicide because they can no longer endure the burden of life and see no other way out of their dilemma. They have used up all of their emotional, spiritual, and mental reserves. Black women seldom commit suicide.

As an African American female pastor and educator, I am frequently asked to serve on boards, speak at conferences, and conduct seminars. Many of the boards I serve on are mostly white; some of them are all African American and sometimes predominantly male. When I meet with the predominantly white boards, I constantly find myself facing racism. When I meet with the all African American, predominantly male boards, I must fight sexism. When I come home, I am often emotionally drained and tempted to give up the fight. But my faith in God, my sense of commitment to a larger struggle, and my communication with other sisters in the struggle cause me to keep up the fight.

Concerning classism, an editorial by David L. Green in *The Philadelphia Inquirer* emphasized the fact that black women are welfare scapegoats. He pointed out that both conservatives and liberals are directing white-middle-class resentment toward black women when they reduce the problem of the poverty of blacks to illegitimacy and welfare dependency while ignoring the existing social and economic realities that contributed to the dilemma of black women. The economic reality of the black woman is that she earns, on an average, less than any other segment in the work force. The social reality is the shrinking pool of marriageable black men. Yet we, black women, press on.

The social reality leads me to coin another "ism" that African American women are forced to live under: "singleism." The shrinking pool of marriageable African American men can be easily documented by the over six hundred thousand African American men in the prison system, the rising violent-death rate of young African American males, and the high rate of unemployment and underemployment. Another phenomenon is the increasing number of highly paid black entertainers and athletes marrying white women. One television commentator referred to this as the "trophy wife." This is interpreted as a subtle message of rejection of the black female by the black male. Yet black women press on.

"From whence cometh this strength?" I can compare it to an anecdote I heard told by a minister. The story goes like this: The minister took his children to the beach one day. They noticed newly hatched baby turtles struggling to get out from under the sand. (Turtles lay their eggs in the sand.) The turtles' destination was the sea. The children felt sorry for the baby turtles and proceeded to help some of the turtles by picking them up and putting them in the ocean.

These baby turtles were soon devoured by the denizens of the sea. But the turtles that were allowed to continue the struggle and make it to the sea on their own strength survived in the sea, for the strength they needed to survive was gained in their struggle.

If this analogy can be applied to African American women, we are the strongest people on this continent! Given all of the facts cited above and according to all psychological theory, black women in America should have the highest rate of suicide, yet we press on and live on. We make up 70 percent of the congregations of our churches. We are the ones holding our homes together. We are willing to work at the most menial jobs to help support our families. We are the ones who attend the parent-teacher meetings. Our strength comes from our struggle. So press on, black women!

Thought for the Day: "Without struggle there is no progress." (Frederick Douglass)

Audrey F. Bronson, D. Min., is an ordained minister and was consecrated as bishop in 1994. She established the Sanctuary Church of the Open Door in 1975 and is also founder of the Sanctuary Christian Academy, the Sanctuary Bible Institute, and the Sanctuary Counseling and Referral Center.

Naomi Tyler-Lloyd Brooks

My Auntie

Ironically, funerals are one of the most popular types of family get-togethers. As I attended my grandmother's funeral in January and shared some precious moments with my "crazy Aunt Phyllis," my spirit grieved with the recognition that soon she would be the guest of honor at another such family gathering. Auntie, a cancer survivor, was beginning to lose her battle.

In the months to come, I would spend hours by the bedside of a woman whose trademark was her incredible mind and watch her winsome wit and clever clauses fade with pronounced progression. This woman, whom I had loved for years and with whom I shared personality traits, could no longer retrieve words or recognize who I was. Fate had forced us into a deeper spiritual relationship that was possible only through our mutual relationship with God.

I would look into her eyes and see her soul. When I could no longer comprehend what she was saying, I had to connect with who she was and what she was communicating. Then it became evident to me that God was dealing and healing, and my spirit was quickened to seek God in a more meaningful way.

On the long drive home, I would process the evenings and simultaneously experience grief and comfort. Knowing what was inevitable was somehow buffered with what was happening to us both. Although I was losing her, I was gaining a part of her that I never had but would always have. Five months later, as I placed flowers on her grave, my eyes shed tears, but my soul was at peace. In her dying, my aunt had given me deeper insight into the relevance of our souls in relationship to God.

Thank you, Lord, for the pains in my life that draw me closer to you. Thank you for speaking peace to my soul.

Thought for the Day: Valleys lead to victories if we allow God to speak peace to us.

Naomi Tyler-Lloyd Brooks received her bachelor's degree from Fairleigh Dickinson University in Rutherford, New Jersey, and her Master of Science in Education from Hunter College in New York City. An accredited alcoholics counselor, she is employed by the Mt. Sinai Medical Center and the Resident Treatment Center.

Nan M. Brown

Redemptive Survival

> *"But as for you, ye thought evil against me; but God meant it unto good, to bring to pass, as it is this day, to save much people alive."* —Genesis 50:20

God does not promise us that the days of our lives will be free from struggles. God does not tell us that we will miraculously escape evil, illness, pain, rejection, disappointments, and suffering, or that trying circumstances, difficulties, or obstacles will be moved out of our way. God does promise, however, that whatever our daily struggles are, he will be with us. We need to always remember God's promises to us because they never fail. God keeps his promises.

This morning I received a call from a sister who was confronted with a situation that she felt she would not be able to survive: she had been denied a position in a church for which she was more than qualified. I praise God for the opportunity to provide words of encouragement and consolation to sisters during these trying times, for I have often cried most of the night due to similar situations. But I have held on to God's words recorded by the psalmist that "weeping may endure for a night, but joy cometh in the morning" (Psalm 30:5b). It is not easy to survive in a seemingly cruel, selfish, and insensitive world. When we trust completely in God and tenaciously hold on, however, we will experience redemptive survival—survival that is liberating, forgiving, and salvific. Not only will we survive life's daily struggles; we will also experience wholeness and liberation that enables us to overcome even more serious obstacles.

Joseph's experience is an excellent example of how God can move in the life of an individual who does not easily give up. When Joseph's brothers stood before the prime minister of Egypt and realized that this man was their brother whom they had sold into slavery twenty years before, they expected words of condemnation. But Joseph said to them, "Fear not: for am I in the place of God? But as for you, ye thought evil against me; but God meant it for good, to bring to pass, as it is this day, to save much people alive" (Genesis 50:19-20).

Joseph experienced redemptive survival. Not only had he survived; he had a heart full of forgiveness. I can identify with Joseph and others who have experienced redemptive survival. I have had to overcome many daily struggles, but thank God, because of my love, faith, and walk with God, I have managed to survive.

One of my greatest disappointments came during my second pastorate, when people whom I loved dearly decided after three years that they preferred I resign. They meant it for evil, but God meant it for good. God gave me a new vision to found a church. I obeyed God's direction, and God blessed me with a beautiful congregation and a new church building. My overcoming of this one ordeal brought about an indescribable redemptive survival in my life.

Thought for the Day: If God be for us, who can be against us? Let nothing separate you from the love of God.

Dr. Nan M. Brown is the founder and senior pastor of The Way of the Cross Baptist Church in Palmyra, Virginia. She holds a B.S. degree from the District of Columbia Teachers College; an M.Div. from the School of Theology, Virginia Union University; and a Doctor of Divinity from the School of Theology, Virginia Union.

Alicia D. Byrd

Family Secrets

Though we keep quiet about it, most of us come from families that bear little resemblance to television's Huxtables or Cleavers. Somewhere in our family line there was physical, substance, or emotional abuse. We come from family systems in which children did not receive the nurturing necessary to develop into adults who are in harmony with themselves and their world.

If your family was marked by a strong need to control the thoughts and actions of family members, a code of silence and denial of family problems, or isolation from the world, yours may have been a dysfunctional family system. In the Bible, we see examples of dysfunctional family systems as we read of Lot's daughters having sexual relations with him (Genesis 19:30-38), a

Corinthian Christian man having an affair with his father's wife (1 Corinthians 5:1), and Ammon raping his sister Tamar (2 Samuel 13:10-14)—to mention a few.

Because of the dysfunction in our families, we adopt certain roles that are passed on to successive generations. While this is painful for those who are honest enough to receive it, sometimes the wound must be opened before it can heal. This is the essence of Exodus 20:5, which talks about the sins of the fathers being visited on the children to the third and fourth generation. Unless life-changing, behavior-altering, mind-transforming salvation comes to us, we will repeat the mistakes of our parents and be shackled just as they were. Our salvation comes as we: (1) Accept that God loves us unconditionally. Sin, not the sinner, is rejected. (2) Accept that abundant life means liberation from self-hatred, loneliness, and the effects of physical, mental, or sexual abuse. With prayer and therapy, we can become the person God meant us to be, freed from the chains of our past. (3) Move forward, living one day at a time. Paul talks about "forgetting what lies behind and straining forward to what lies ahead" (Philippians 3:13, NRSV). While the past cannot be erased, we can learn from the experiences of others and free ourselves from the chains that have bound us. Prayer, acceptance of our past, counseling with a therapist skilled in working with dysfunctional families, a program of spiritual development, and making a commitment to ourselves to do what is necessary to live abundantly, however long it takes, will put us on the path of freedom and liberation.

God is in the saving and delivering business and does not want us to remain in bondage. It takes courage to change and grow, but God has given us Holy Spirit power to overcome difficulties, problems, and limitations, so that nothing can hinder us from living the abundant life Christ gives to us.

Thought for the Day: God can set us free!

Rev. Alicia D. Byrd, Ph.D., is pastor of the St. Stephens African Methodist Episcopal Church in Elkridge, Maryland, and is on the staff of the Congress of National Black Churches, Washington, D.C.

Vivian Campbell-Mack

Through a Loss, God Gave Life

God is faithful. I've tried him and known him and found him to be a friend. Ain't no doubt about it, on God you can depend!

This particular lesson began in 1991 when someone very dear and close to me, my mother, was suddenly diagnosed with liver and bone cancer. Speak of devastation—more like a catastrophe! She was not just my mother but my best friend. I always confided in her; I always wanted to know her opinions, and her approval was very important to me. I admired her honesty, courage, and amazing strength.

There wasn't much time to prepare for my mother's death. She died exactly three weeks from the time I found out about her illness.

While I did not know during those weeks what the outcome would be, I did know that I had to trust God. I began to seek him during that time, praying for understanding and insight to see his goodness in the midst of this situation. Through reading God's Word, the Bible, God began to show me his promises. I saw how others were brought through situations even more devastating than mine, and I began to trust that God would see me through, too, because God is faithful—God will do what he says he'll do. Didn't God do it for Abraham, the first father of faith? Didn't God do it for us in giving us his only begotten Son, Jesus? There is no greater love!

Knowing God's promises, I knew how much more he would do for me. I began to be encouraged and found a sustaining strength that only God could give. God gave me an understanding that surpassed all understanding. God gave me a joy—an unspeakable joy—the kind only God could give.

It was not easy getting to this point in my life—and it's still a struggle. I had to go through circumstances in which I had to step out in faith—and as I took one step, God took two. There will come a time in your life when you will have to choose either to step out in faith—trusting, leaning, and depending on God—or lean on your own understanding. Choose God's way; it is the best way.

In 1992 one of my prayers for the new year was, "Lord, please let death pass my door." God's answer: "I'm going to give you life." In November of that year, my daughter was born. God had not only spared me another experience with death but had given me life and restored my loss with a new relationship—a new mother-and-daughter relationship. Isn't God faithful? I've tried him and I know him. I've found him to be my friend—and on him I will depend!

Thought for the Day: God is a life-giving stream. Today I will count life, not my losses.

Vivian Campbell-Mack is a member of Mariners' Temple Baptist Church in New York City, where she serves in the teaching and music ministries.

Delores H. Carpenter

Walking Together in Sisterhood

Tell me, where do we go? Whom can we count on? Who dries our tears?

It sure is hard to find men who are completely comfortable having us around. We are still viewed as liabilities, even after all these years of working side by side with them, or working behind the scenes to encourage and comfort. Why is reciprocity so difficult? Is it because of the political cost of breaking away from the "old-boys network" by affirming a woman pastor?

Women ministers are still marginalized, still lack full collegiality. Often, it is subtle. The men will never mention it, and you are not to take it personally. But something is missing. The laughter may cease when you enter. Clergy, as a professional group, are divided and alienated from one another. Alienation from one another eventually leads to insufficient affirmation, and lack of affirmation leads to alienation from one's self. I still groan as I listen to the groans of my female students who want answers to hard questions.

My own study of black women in ministry reveals that only 30 percent are married, and not all of these marriages are as fulfilling as one would hope. Many of these women are divorced, separated, or widowed. Many are raising children without a father in the home. Where do these women turn for support, nurture, and intimacy?

I see two signs of hope on the horizon. The first comes from younger male ministers who study with women seminarians on a daily basis. As a result, they are developing a genuine appreciation for women's ministerial gifts, aspirations, and commitments. Of course, because seminaries are liberal forums, some say only what they think their professors (some of whom are women) and the women students want to hear, while they sing another tune when they are under the tutelage of traditional, older gatekeepers of the faith. They question how politically correct "pushing women" is in the wider context of the church—where they hope to set the world on fire. In spite of this reality, there is a critical mass who have emerged as friends and true colleagues, those men who take an honest stand and dialogue with women in ways that count. Increasingly, they are willing to work beside women and, in rare instances, even take on this assignment as a cause.

Of even greater potential is the way a new sisterhood is emerging. Women are helping other women and thus gaining energy for themselves. They are forming close relationships of trust and are learning how to depend on one another. This is not new, but it is increasingly more valued, especially by older women who are beyond the child-rearing years and are seeking strength in one another. For every single woman minister who bears the burdens of human souls and the conflicts of struggling churches, it is essential that some good, solid friendships undergird her sanity. Such relationships restore balance and wholeness to our fragmented, misunderstood lives.

Today I stop and give thanks for our true partners in ministry.

Thought for the Day: Walk together, children, and don't get weary!

Rev. Dr. Delores H. Carpenter is an associate professor of religious education at Howard University School of Divinity as well as the pastor of Michigan Park Christian Church (Disciples of Christ) in Washington, D.C. She earned a B.A. from Morgan State University, an M.Div. from Howard University School of Divinity, an M.A. from Washington University, and a Doctorate of Education from Rutgers University.

Henrietta Carter

The Child of a King

"Listen, my son, to your father's instruction and do not forsake your mother's teaching. They will be a garland to grace your head and a chain to adorn your neck." —Proverbs 1:8-9 (NIV)

I sit in your presence, my son, and I feel your pain at being a black man in a society that regards neither your blackness nor your manhood, and I ache within—desperately searching for something, anything to say that will assure you that you are an African American prince, descendant of African kings, created by God, who is the Father and Mother of all humankind.

My son, you are the child of a King!

Royalty, my son, that is what you are.

My son, I gaze upon your dark, young, handsome face, already etched with the pain of being a black man in a world that rejects your uniqueness, and I long to comfort you, to hold you, and, yes, to guide you to Jesus, who alone gives the promise of God's acceptance to all who will believe and receive him.

My son, you are the chosen of God!

Unique, my son, that's what you are.

Daily, my son, I talk with you, and I hear the agony in your voice as you struggle to make sense of a world's senseless violence. I yearn to give you the security and peace you are searching for, to somehow help you understand that even amid the chaos, God is.

Jesus, my son, is your security.

Jesus, my son, is your peace.

My son, I walk with you through the Harlem streets, and in your silence I sense your lostness at having experienced the loss of so many of your childhood friends to addiction, prison, and even death. And I, in my own silence, offer up my prayer to God that God will be gracious to you, help you rise above the here and now, and give you the vision of the prophets, the dreams of the wise, and the understanding of the learned.

My son, in your silence see Jesus.

In your lostness, look up.
In your uniqueness, thank God.
In your maleness, stand tall.
Of your blackness, be proud.
For your heritage, praise God!

Thought for the Day: My son, it is an honor to be your parent.

Rev. Henrietta Carter is the assistant pastor of Mariners' Temple Baptist Church in New York City. In 1990 she was named Teacher of the Year by the New York City Board of Education for her outstanding leadership. She earned a B.A. from Hunter College, an M.S. in Education from Hunter College, and an M.Div. from New York Theological Seminary.

Cheryl Price Clemetson

Peace in the Midst of a Storm

> *"Peace I leave with you, My peace I give to you; not as the world gives do I give to you. Let not your heart be troubled, neither let it be afraid." —John 14:27 (NKJV)*

Every now and then we are given the opportunity to learn more about God's peace in the midst of what appears to be a hopeless situation. That time came for me when my mother, Vivian Price, had a terminal illness called Addison's disease. Yet in spite of her daily suffering and pain, she had more faith, integrity, and inner strength than anyone I've ever met. Hers was not the peace gained from daily medication or operations that are supposed to make things better but the peace of Jesus Christ.

One day, as she lay peacefully on her hospital bed, the doctors told my father and the rest of the family they did not know if she would make it through the night. My father had developed a quiet inner strength of his own that let us know he was able to give his wife support and love and was prepared for whatever would happen. But I did not have that same peace or strength. I had prayed and prayed and prayed and prayed for my mother's healing. I had lit candles, made the sign of the cross on her forehead, read every Scripture I knew about healing, and listened to the "healing preachers." Yet she was not getting any better; she was not miraculously healed.

As she lay on her "bed of affliction," my mother helped me to realize that we can have true peace in the midst of a storm. She must have seen the worried look on my face, or heard the quiet prayers that I spoke, or felt the anxiety in my hands as I touched her brow. Whatever it was, I will always remember how she turned, looked up at me, and said, "Cheryl, I am at peace. I have made peace with God. Everything is going to be all right."

At that moment, I realized that everything

would be all right. My mother, who was sick, was telling me that she had peace within her and I did not have to worry. She had a peace that no one could give her or take away from her. Even when the storms of life were raging, she could still be at peace with the Lord. And so could I.

When life is raging all around you, remember to meditate on the peace that Jesus extends to each of us if we are willing to ride through the storm with him.

Dear Heavenly Peacemaker, give us the courage and strength to ride with you through the storms of our lives, so that we can have the peace that only you can give.

Thought for the Day: Peace, be still!

Dr. Cheryl Price Clemetson is an associate minister of the Metropolitan Baptist Church in Washington, D.C. She received an M.Div. and a Ph.D. from the Colgate Rochester Divinity School.

Doris W. Dennard

Eliminating Negative Clutter

When Jesus taught us to forgive unconditionally, he did not mean that women should
passively tolerate being abused mentally,
physically, emotionally, and spiritually. We
were not created to abuse ourselves or to place
ourselves or our children in bondage to alcohol
or drugs in response to the maltreatment of
others. The Scriptures teach the importance of
freeing the mind from all thoughts that keep us
from being the power-filled reservoirs that we
were created to be and to become. We must
learn to make a receptive home for the creative
ideas of God in our minds, hearts, souls, and
everyday lives in order to actualize the lasting
spiritual empowerment in our affairs.

If we allow our minds to remain cluttered with nightmares about present and past hurts and abuses, we are not choosing to concentrate on healing ourselves. Until our minds are free from negative clutter, we keep on exposing ourselves to situations and relationships that continue to hurt and keep us in bondage to our afflictions and addictions.

We have been blessed with the gift of creative imagination, which is the channel for receptivity to the mind of God. We can replace hostile, dependent, bitter, resentful, jealous, hurt, worried thoughts with thoughts of healing our minds, hearts, and lives. We can rid ourselves of relations that inflict pain, misery, and insult upon us by learning to establish a living, power-filled, faith-filled relationship with the Spirit of Life!

Day by day, we can eliminate negative clutter by choosing to concentrate on "whatever is true, whatever is noble, whatever is right, whatever is pure, whatever is lovely, whatever is admirable" (Philippians 4:8, NIV).

We can use positive affirmations such as the following: "I choose to entertain creative thoughts throughout this day. The Spirit of Life fills me with good ideas and helps me to put them in action!"

Thought for the Day: "This is the day the LORD has made; let us rejoice and be glad in it" (Psalm 118:24).

Doris W. Dennard, ACSW, DCSW, is assistant director and a cofounder of Harlem Interfaith Counseling Services (HICS), Inc., in Central Harlem, a licensed family mental health clinic. She dedicates her meditation to all women, but especially to women of African-Edenic descent who are a part of the life of the Harlem community.

Valerie K. Eley

Don't Let the Busyness Fool You

"*A woman named Martha received him into her house. And she had a sister called Mary, who sat at the Lord's feet and listened to his teaching. But Martha was distracted with much serving; and she went to him and said, 'Lord, do you not care that my sister has left me to serve alone? Tell her then to help me.' But the Lord answered her, 'Martha, Martha, you are anxious and troubled about many things; one thing is needful. Mary has chosen the good portion, which shall not be taken away from her.'*"
—*Luke 10:38-42 (RSV)*

Teach us, dear God, to have compassion on the Marthas of this world who often make life a little brighter and more hospitable for the Marys. For we confess that if we received notice that you were going to pay us a visit, we too would want to make sure that everything was in perfect order. But help us also to remember that the Supernatural will not be entertained by natural ways.

Grace us with the wisdom, dear God, to be still, to sit at your feet, and to prepare to have our bodies fed and our houses cleansed when you favor us with your presence. We thank you for the reminder that you do not require us to put everything in order before inviting you in. We recognize that you are the One who straightens everything up, and you, through the power of the Holy Ghost, are the One who cleanses and purifies, sterilizes and makes brand new.

Thank you, Lord, that spending time with you builds a defense against anything that anybody tries to say about us, and protects us from anything that anybody tries to do to us. We are strengthened in knowing that "no weapon that is formed against us will prosper" and that "every tongue that rises against us in judgment will be condemned." We know, beyond the shadow of any doubt, that whatever humanity means for evil, you have the power to use for our good. If we worship you, like Mary, and sit at your feet, you have promised to make our enemies our footstool.

Finally, God, we thank you that we don't have to prove anything to anybody. We claim the victory in knowing that righteousness is about relationship and not deeds, and we are confident this day that if we have the proper relationship with you, the proper deeds will also follow.

Thought for the Day: Jesus does not require us to put everything in order before inviting him in. Sit at his feet and be blessed.

Minister Valerie K. Eley is a native of Newport News, Virginia. She is a former Benjamin E. Mays Scholar and a graduate of Smith College in Massachusetts. She received her M.Div. from the New York Theological Seminary.

Rosa V. Ferguson-James

Building Positive Race Relations

<====>

> *"So Naomi returned together with Ruth the Moabite, her daughter-in-law, who came back with her from the country of Moab." —Ruth 1:22a (NRSV)*

As the story unfolds in the book of Ruth, we find two women who were leaders in their own right—"sheroes," if you will. Naomi had heard that the economy and living conditions in Judah had improved; there was food in the land again. So she proposed that her daughters-in-law, Ruth and Orpah, now widows, return to their own families, and she would go back to hers. Orpah obeyed. But Ruth made the tremendous declaration of commitment, love, loyalty, and willingness to adjust in a foreign land as she said, "Do not press me to leave you or to turn back from following you!" (Ruth 1:16, NRSV).

Although we hear often of Ruth's loyalty to Naomi, there is no question of Naomi's similar loyalty to her husband and sons as she assumes the role of wife, mother, and caregiver when the family moved to Moab. Nor is there any question about her survival skills and her "motherwit" as she made a home for her family in this strange land of Moab or later gave directions to Ruth for wooing Ruth's second husband, Boaz.

But let us reflect for a moment and try to feel what Naomi must have felt long ago as she embarked on her journey from her home to Moab. Think about this Judean stranger, this young wife, who feels compelled to leave her home—her relatives, her Women's Mission Circle, her Sunday school class, her support system—to seek sustenance in a foreign country. Then imagine how it must have felt to encounter one tragedy after another. Some of us can relate and share similar stories. Indeed, she was left desolate and lonely. I suspect that Naomi had flashbacks of her early years when she watched her sons grow and marry women who were of a different faith and culture, people whose roots emanated from an incestuous relationship between Lot and his daughter. Her memories surely would have included times when she could not figure out the foreign foods, the customs, or the values of this new land.

Ruth, on the other hand, is commended for her faith and actions. But we must also note that she had Naomi to emulate as she assimilated into Judean culture and religion. Ruth could learn proper protocol simply by watching Naomi. She could ask questions about things she did not understand and raise concerns about strange ways with Naomi, her mother-in-law and mentor. Naomi had had no one—no one with a command of the customs and a familiarity with the people.

Despite their differences—age, appearance, religion, culture—Naomi was still able to embrace Ruth's country and its people. She convinced her friends, neighbors, and daughters-in-law that she knew how to live so as to accept and be accepted by others as fellow citizens and to see God as her guiding force. Naomi could have responded to her situation by stating, "I am not of the same race or religion as these people in Moab, so I will keep my distance and not mix." Like many of us in America today, she could have used race and culture as a reason for separation rather than as an opportunity to learn about one another and express our racial and cultural diversity. (Nelson Mandela has shown the world how to use race as a means to bring about reconciliation.)

Like women in our world on the brink of the twenty-first century, Naomi could have concentrated on survival and the scarcity of resources to feed the hungry. She could have cited statistics of family crises similar to those that tell of our own children wounded and murdered on the streets. Surely the abuse and the neglect of children was just as despicable then as now. There is no question that abusive relationships existed. Naomi wanted to prevent further family breakdown and family crises, so she sent the young women to their own families.

God honored Naomi because of her bridge-building skills, her willingness to dialogue with Moabites such as Ruth and Orpah. In that environment of reconciliation, God honored her willingness to move from the role of a stranger and sojourner in the land to that of a significant family member. And as Naomi showed this pioneering spirit, this endurance for hardships, this perseverance and vision, we also lift up African American women like Ida B. Wells-Barnett, who cofounded the NAACP, and Nannie Helen Burroughs, who served as president of the women's auxiliary of the National Baptist Convention, U.S.A., Inc. and founded a school for women and girls when she was denied a teaching position in Washington, D.C., because of her race.

Yes, God's highest honor given to Naomi and Ruth was to place them in the lineage of Jesus the Christ. As he did with Naomi and our ancestors, God will honor us as we feed those who are hungry, as we visit and care for the sick, as we generate a passion that causes us to act on behalf of children. God honors us as we appreciate one another's individuality and diversity. God honors us when we have a zeal for the reduction and elimination of economic and psychological deprivation. God honors us as we take personal and corporate responsibility and work diligently toward the goal of safe homes, safe schools, safe communities, and safe churches.

Thought for the Day: May we honor God and be faithful this day, as God honors us and is faithful to us.

Rosa V. Ferguson-James, Ed.D., is the principal of James Madison Middle School in Oakland, California. She is vice-president of American Baptist Churches of the West and a member of the board of directors for Green Lake Conference Center. She is a member of the Beth Eden Baptist Church in Oakland, California.

Cora Fields

Listening to Our Children

Most of us really talk a good talk, but we refuse to listen and set forth an action plan that produces results and alternatives. What we don't realize is that listening carefully is something we can do to overcome the neglect of our youth. In many cases, children have come out of homes where true parenting never existed. The future of our communities depends on our honest commitment to investing in our youth without a lot of rhetoric. We must give them a sense of hope. We have the knowledge but lack action. Just talking will not carry us intelligently into the twenty-first century. We must begin to listen.

Listening is not something we've been trained to do, but we can begin by saying to ourselves,

"I will listen." We must practice active listening on a daily basis until it becomes a habit. The art of listening allows us to learn and to respond intelligently. We also show respect for others as we listen, and we grow immensely as we interact with others.

As we listen to our youth, their eyes, tone of voice, and body language will deliver clear messages. When I speak to youngsters in various churches, youth centers, and schools, I also listen carefully. I encourage them to see the value of discipline and hard work, for I know this will increase their self-esteem.

How dare we allow our children to be classified as dysfunctional! Of course there's work to be done! Of course we're tired! So what? No one else is going to take control of them if we don't. Is being tired something new?

Consider investing in one youngster rather than complaining. Give your time to a young family member or a young person from the community. Don't procrastinate; just do it. Begin now to listen to the children. Each of us possesses something we can share with them—a smile, a pleasant voice, something to pass on. We must seek not to judge or condemn but to be quick to listen, slow to speak, slow to anger, realizing we each come with a gift for another.

We all have times when we are troubled and confused by the daily challenges of life, but despair need never be the end. You see, the end is God's loving care, for faith is the "substance of things hoped for, the evidence of things not seen" (Hebrews 11:1). We must give our children this sense of hope—the same kind of spiritual hope that you and I have experienced with our extended families. Leave no room for doubt or fear, mothers, fathers, sisters, brothers, aunts, and uncles. In the midst of the many problems that plague us, stand tall, remain firm in faith, and listen to the words of Jesus from Mark 5:34: "Daughter, thy faith hath made thee whole; go in peace."

Thought for the Day: Children are a blessing from the Lord.

Cora Fields was formerly the associate director for management training for New York Telephone and is currently a member of the New York Historical Society and the New York Botanical Gardens, a life member of the NAACP and the National Council of Negro Women, and a member of the friends of CUNY (City University of New York) and the New York Society of Performance and Instruction.

Jami Floyd

Choosing to Be African American

My mother is standing in the nine-items-or-less line at the crowded Sloan's supermarket on the Lower East Side of Manhattan. She is waiting for me, her teenage daughter, to run and get an item we'd forgotten. The old man behind my mother is joking with my mother about the crowds at the market on Sundays. As I step into line next to my mother, his expression changes as he sees my mother standing next to a daughter of a different race—me. Even after thirteen years of raising me and years of experiences just like this one, my mother is angry and looks away to try to contain her anger. Years later we will laugh about "that crazy man at Sloan's."

I am black. My mother is white. "Black" is

how my country labels me. "African American" is how I have chosen to define myself. I am comfortable and secure in my African American "label," although I bemoan, now and again, the existence of such cognitive labeling systems in our "free society."

Of course, my mixed heritage is really not that unusual. Couplings between men and women of different races, like that between my white (Anglo Saxon) mother and my black (Native and African American) father, are an age-old phenomenon, in spite of the taboo they carry in American psychology, culture, and media. (Consider, for example, Marc Antony and Cleopatra.) The United States is much more a land of mixed heritage than we Americans care to admit.

But I am grounded, historically and otherwise, in this heritage. Ever since childhood, I have felt that my parents' union (they have been married for thirty-eight years) and my very existence are symbols of what we as a society can be once we get past our race differences and look to our commonality as human beings. Some white folks often express difficulty in understanding my African American self-identification as positive rather than negative. They see it as a rejection of my white mother and her history and identity, and of White America in general. As I probe a little deeper in conversations with these folks, it often becomes apparent that what they don't understand is why I would define myself as African American. Why wouldn't I instead define myself as white? "After all, wouldn't anyone?" they seem to be asking.

Several of my close friends are also children born of interracial marriages. One night some of these friends and I are hanging out at my place. I relate one of the above-described conversations that I'd had that morning with a white colleague. Not surprisingly, my friends explain that they have had similar conversations with white folks. Unlike my white colleague, these friends know exactly where I am coming from, and I know where they're coming from. We do not reject or deny our white parentage or heritage, although many of us do not know our white relatives—apart from the white parent who raised us. In my own case, my mother's family—with the exception of her own mother, who lived with us when I was a girl—essentially disowned her for marrying a black man. In 1956, the year my parents married, a white Texas belle simply did not marry a black football player/artist. These friends and I marvel at the inability of whites to conceive why we would want to see ourselves as people of color and as African Americans.

But there are exceptions; some white folks do get it. And my mother is one of them. My mother had a strong enough sense of self to allow me to determine who and what I was going to be. And in the end, my pride in being African American brings me closer to my mother. This identity gives me a stronger sense of history and of self with which I come to my relationship with my mother, thereby ensuring that race never gets in the way of that relationship.

My mother taught me that "difference" is a positive, a strength, rather than something strange or exotic. She taught me that there is strength in a multicultural society and that each of us makes a contribution as part of that multicultural society. This is part of the richness of our lives.

My mother understood that I needed to be exposed to a diverse group of role models—and African American role models in particular. She made certain that these were available to me. And she did not attempt to stand in as a surrogate for them. My mother also taught me that as an African American, I am the descendant of people who built America and made it the great and prosperous land that this country has become.

My African ancestors arrived on these shores generations ago, and their contribution to this land leaves me (and my children and grandchildren) as entitled as any other American to a piece of the American dream. Of course, this is an important lesson for a black child to understand in a society that so often denies African Americans their share in the American dream.

I kept a journal as a teenager. In it I wrote down something my mother once explained: "It would have been a mistake to delude you into thinking you could be anything other than black in this country. Besides, nothing other than what you are would be any more desirable." I think that, for my mother, parenthood is much more than a domestic rite of passage. For my mother, motherhood has always been grass-roots political work—work for which she has always been willing to swim upstream against the tide of popular opinion. I don't think she sees it as hard work, however. In fact, she talks often about how Black America and the multiculturalism of her community have expanded, and continue to expand, her own mind and life.

Today, as two adults, my mother and I talk about race, racism, and race politics. We talk about race as society projects race and racial stereotypes on us. We joke about the man at the supermarket and other similar incidents. We argue sometimes, but we don't get hung up on it. At times when our differences in age and race become apparent in how we perceive the world and our places in it, the differences don't detract from our love and trust. Besides, my mother always says that you can't expect a person who has had different life experiences to see the world the way you do, even if that person is your mother or your daughter.

My mother is my mother, and I am very protective of her and my relationship with her. I often find myself in a strange bind—the bind of explaining that I am black and my mother is white. Negotiating this is one of life's little challenges. But day to day, my mother and I are simply two women making our way in the world: going to work, worrying about our weight and our health, fighting off the flu that's going around, dealing with our latest fender bender or parking ticket, arguing with our husbands about watching too much football. At thirty, I have begun to see my mother in myself: we share similar political outlooks, we both love old mystery and horror movies, we're both light sleepers, and we both love coffee. And the shape of our faces is the same. But, of course, it always has been.

Thought for the Day: I love who I am.

Jami Floyd is a teaching fellow at Stanford Law School in California. A native of New York, she recently completed a White House fellowship, where she served with Vice-President Al Gore. She is married and lives in the Bay Area.

Ruby Brent Ford

Amazing Grace

Great women's organizations have been a dynamic force within social movements, religious and educational work, business and professional ventures, and all efforts facing humankind. Yet the woman's role has been defined in the world as a place of little significance by various cultures, and great women and their achievements are spoken of much less than the works of great men. Nevertheless, African American women have used their belief in God and God's "amazing grace" to overcome the double burdens of racial and sexual discrimination. We have gone from being field hands to being boardroom chairpersons on Wall Street and in corporate America.

Although little was recorded about women's organizations, almost all of them were connected to the church. The church was the focal point for schooling, social activities, recreation, and organizational activities—and women were the early fund-raisers and public-relations persons.

Black women's organizations today are of every description and historic origin. What is the message that the present-day women's organizations want to convey? We hear messages about how to work with a team and how to assume responsibility for carrying out the mandate and cause of the organization, as well as how to network and work together for a better tomorrow. Many women's organizations and movements are doing well in aiding the communities through social action, politics, and economics.

Yet moral decay is everywhere. There must be a return to the church. We must make a great effort to turn again to God in order to deal with needs: family and marriage relationships, jobs, money, health, education, and children. Our women's organizations must reflect on past successes by acknowledging God and looking forward to new horizons of good fortune and fulfillment of their purposes through the power and grace of the Lord Jesus Christ.

Thought for the Day: Today I recommit to the old landmark, the church of Jesus Christ, which has been there for me and the women I know.

Ruby Brent Ford is an active senior citizen in the New York City civic arena. A member of the New York Coalition of 100 Black Women and a member of the Bridge Street A.M.E. Church in Brooklyn, New York, she is an inspiration and mentor to many women.

Maxine Foster-Durham

The Presence of God to Deliver

"And Moses said to the people, 'Fear not, stand firm, and see the salvation of the LORD, which he will work for you today . . .' Then Miriam, the prophetess, the sister of Aaron, took a timbrel in her hand; and all the women went out after her with timbrels and dancing. And Miriam sang to them: 'Sing to the LORD, for he has triumphed gloriously; the horse and his rider he has thrown into the sea.'" —Exodus 14:13; 15:20-21

These verses describe the awesome events that set the stage for Israel's liberation. Yet what a request, given the circumstances! Behind Israel approaches an army of Egyptians—chariots, horses, and horsemen—and before them appears a spectacular sight: the waters of the sea roll back, forming a wall on either side of the pathway and creating a "dry highway in the midst of a wet sea." The challenge was to stand firm. This would have hardly been a time for me to stand firm! I would have either been trembling in fear or falling on the ground in awe of Yahweh's presence and power to deliver! Yet are we not today sometimes confronted by circumstances that both startle us by their unexpected timing and perplex us by their inequity?

Women, like the Israelites, are experiencing great persecution at the hands of those who, like Pharaoh, are eager to consciously perpetuate their enslavement. No one can deny that women are, in a real sense, a displaced people in search of a place to be all that God has called and compelled them to be, disenfranchised due to the popular belief that their place is to be in the home and their role is to meet everyone else's needs. We are bombarded with issues: the right to work or remain at home (without experiencing guilt in either case); the right to elect choice or life; the right to exist as created in the image and likeness of God and declared good or to experience the denial of that right to exist, plagued by the demons of denigrating sexual, verbal, and physical abuse. When women refuse to become punching bags, to accept lewd behavior, or to be recipients of foul language and its emotional scars, we are labeled as "feminist" or "womanist" and accused of trampling on the power pavilions of men. We are heralded as too powerful or too strong, and somehow that has become equated with being domineering and translated as negative. Yet power and strength are necessary for these times and must not be misconstrued as negative.

My sisters, our deliverance from the plagues that seek our demise is linked to our obedience to move at God's command and not shrink back in fear to the enslavement of the times. Times are crucial as we witness sisters enslaved for their belief in God's call upon their lives, blatantly told to be silent. Even though strides have been achieved in the church arena, the accomplishments are not noble enough or substantial enough to allow the churches acquittal.

We affirm that God can do anything but fail. Thus our response, in humble obedience, is to move forward into the murky waters of uncertainty, not always sure that our feet will not slip or that the ground will remain dry. Yet the movement is with the understanding that God has proclaimed victory, that God will be glorified, and that God's victory is already accomplished. Faith requires that we walk into our Red Sea, for at the end of the sea deliverance waits.

Thought for the Day: Today I will move forward and see that God has saved me.

Rev. Maxine Foster-Durham is a resident of Connecticut, where she serves as an associate minister of the First Baptist Church of Milford. Rev. Foster-Durham earned the Master of Divinity degree from Princeton Theological Seminary and the S.T.M. degree from the Yale Divinity School.

Sheila Denise Grimes

Watching the Children Grow

> *"Lo, children are an heritage of the LORD: and the fruit of the womb is his reward."* —*Psalm 127:3*

God has blessed me to conceive, bear, and raise four wonderful children. In a span of thirteen years, I gave birth to Adrianne, now twenty-three; Tonisha, sixteen; Chareece, fifteen; and Douglas III, ten. As a parent who stayed at home until all of my own children entered school, I had the opportunity to help raise a number of other children from my community. And for the past four years, I have also watched the children of the church grow as I've served as a minister to children.

Yes, I have watched the children grow, and in

so doing, I bear witness to the truth that "children are an heritage of the Lord." As a caretaker of God's children, I have been given a charge to train up the children in the way they should go; and when they grow older—through prayer, love, hope, faith, spiritual awareness, discipline, patience, and the knowledge of the will of God for their life—my prayer is that they will not depart from it. My work is to lay a foundation as I watch the children grow.

What should that foundation look like?

It should contain prayer, which is direct communication with God. Children should learn at a very early age to pray and give thanks to God for life, health, and strength.

Teaching a child about faith teaches them to know that "faith is the substance of things hoped for, the evidence of things not seen" (Hebrews 11:1).

Spiritual awareness enables a child to see that Jesus loves them and to know that the Bible tells them so. Children know when they are loved and by whom. Teaching the importance of love is the greatest commandment God has given unto us: "Thou shalt love the Lord thy God with all thy heart, and with all thy soul, and with all thy mind. This is the first and greatest commandment" (Matthew 22:37-38). Then our children will be able to love others as they have learned to love themselves.

With love comes discipline. Children learn to respect and honor those who take time to diligently and lovingly correct them when they are wrong and to show them the right way to go.

Discipline will teach patience, not only to the children but to the one who is disciplining. Raising children brings pain and heartache, but as parents or guardians, we "glory in tribulations also: knowing that tribulation worketh patience; And patience, experience; and experience hope" (Romans 5:3-4).

In hope children learn that "I can do all things through Christ which strengtheneth me" (Philippians 4:13). As the children grow, they will learn to build their hope on "nothing less than Jesus' blood and righteousness" and realize that the will of God is for them to accept him as Lord and Savior and trust in him fully, leaning not to their own understanding but in all their ways acknowledging him (see Proverbs 3:5-6).

In watching the children grow, one day we must let them go. As stewards over children, after we lay a firm foundation, all we can do is pray that God will direct their paths and that they will stay in the will of God.

Thought for the Day: Thank you, God, for children. I will enjoy caring for them and watching them grow.

Minister Sheila Denise Grimes, a member of Mariners' Temple Baptist Church in New York City, serves in the ministries of administration, children and special projects. She was graduated from the College of New Rochelle in New Rochelle, New York, with a B.A. in psychology and religious studies, and is pursuing an M.Div. at New York Theological Seminary.

Marcia A. Harris

Determination and Dignity

◧◖◎◖▓◖◎◗◨

Picture: A six-year-old girl standing over an open grave and asking to go in.

Picture: Two years later, an eight-year-old child still asking her grandmother why Momma had to die.

Picture: A ten-year-old girl ecstatic at having passed the common entrance examination in Jamaica, enabling her to go to high school (an earned privilege reserved for the top 40 percent of the population).

Picture: A twelve-year-old being invested as a Master Guide, the highest level of Pathfinder Club (the Seventh-Day Adventist equivalent of the Girl Scouts)—the youngest, not only on the island of Jamaica, but in the world.

Picture: A fourteen-year-old getting a standing

ovation after having played the entire score of the "Ruth and Naomi" Easter cantata on an old pump organ for the choir's performance.

Picture: A sixteen-year-old starting college in a new country and being the only black person as well as the only woman in most of her classes.

Picture: Reality setting in and, after changing her major four times, going back to what she was best at in the first place—chemistry, mathematics, physics, and other sciences.

Picture: Medical school in Washington Heights, relating to and getting to know everyone from the janitors to the dean—and learning from and being inspired by all.

Picture: Her onslaught on the great white mecca on Manhattan's East Side—the first black woman ever to be accepted in the residency program.

Picture: Starting her practice and being told she would not make it in New York City as a gynecologist because she didn't do abortions.

Yes, determination coupled with consummate faith and instilled pride—and underwritten by intense desire—has brought me this far. Life has not been easy. The deck was stacked against me early on, as it is and has been for so many of us. The road is not straight. It has many curves and detours and has been unusually long and hard.

Even adversity, however, can be used to our advantage, as long as we don't lose sight of our goals.

I see in our society today a lack of pride—pride in ourselves, our heritage, our work, our very being. I am referring to the type of pride that merges with humility to become dignity, the pride that is the enforcer of self-imposed standards of character. This pride doesn't make one haughty; it makes one not settle for less than one's capabilities.

We must also have faith: faith in ourselves, in people, in God. We have to believe that our future is in our hands and that we are masters of our fate. Life is not static but is a dynamic process that is constantly changing. Our hopes, desires, and dreams change on a daily, monthly, yearly basis. Our faith enables us to keep things in perspective—and to change that perspective as we need to in order to work things through.

For so many of us, a key ingredient in our support system is someone to give encouragement, someone to believe in us—although ultimately we must believe in ourselves. I am grateful for all my "surrogate mothers," the women who encouraged me after my mother's death. Their encouragement and their faith in me ignited my faith in myself. They not only made me aware of what was expected of me; they instilled in me the belief that I could do anything I wanted to do, that hard work and fortitude eventually pays off, and that obstacles are actually placed in the way not to deter us but to give us something to overcome.

I am also grateful for my daughter, Dana Marie, whom I don't take time to affirm as often as I should. It is my hope that our relationship will continue to grow during her teenage years and that she will benefit from the example I have tried to set and will have garnered the strength, willpower, self-confidence, faith, and pride necessary to see her through life's journey. With God's help, I hope I will always be there for her, as God and the many women of faith were for me.

Thought for the Day: "It's no secret what God can do; what God's done for others, he will do for you."

Marcia A. Harris, M.D., L.H.D. (Hon.), is from the West Indian island of Jamaica. She earned a bachelor's degree in chemistry from Pace University and a medical degree from Columbia University. Dr. Harris maintains a thriving obstetrics/gynecology private practice on Manhattan's East Side. She is active inside and outside of the Seventh-Day Adventist church, speaking frequently to ladies' groups and adolescents.

Elizabeth Harrison Hicks

A Promise to Remember

"But godliness is profitable unto all things, having promise of the life that now is, and of that which is to come."
—*1 Timothy 4:8*

As a little girl of preschool age growing up in Selma, Alabama, I spent much of my time on the farm with my paternal grandparents, Osborne and Ritter Steele, to whom I always referred as "Big Daddy" and "Big Mama." I especially enjoyed visiting the farm during late autumn, after the cotton had been picked and the vegetables and fruits harvested. With most of the field work completed, this meant that seasonal chores would now be centered on the house and barnyard.

Watching my endless, energetic movements became the self-assigned chore and joy of my grandparents.

Often when they were caught up on their work, Big Daddy and Big Mama would hitch a ride with anyone from "The Bend" who happened to be going into Selma. I always made the return trip to the farm with them. Knowing that Mama loved earth-parched peanuts or ash-roasted sweet potatoes as her nightly snack, my grandparents always brought a sack of the freshly gathered produce along.

Years later, I still vividly recall the greeting ritual that I performed whenever my grandparents visited. I always gave Big Mama a gigantic hug, while at the same time leaping for Big Daddy's neck, straddling my legs around his waist, and eliciting a promise from him that I would be included in the return to the family farm. Oh, how I loved those two people who always made me feel so special! Daddy and Mama always let me visit with them for a few days.

Autumn on the farm was as exciting to me as a trip to Disney World is to a four-year-old today. I cherished the private moments shared with my grandparents as we sat around the fireplace popping corn and turning "hoe cakes." Big Daddy told stories of his boyhood adventures as he repaired cane-back chairs or whittled a piece of wood and Big Mama pieced a quilt or made straw brooms—all from light given from kerosene lamps, since electricity was not yet available in that part of the county.

Equally as exciting as those intimate moments with my grandparents were those shared with nearby neighbors and surrounding community members. Every autumn, soon after the sweet potatoes had been banked, corn sent to the miller, and sugar cane made into molasses, a cow and a hog were ceremonially slaughtered. A markswoman with a twenty-two rifle, Big Mama had the task of shooting the boar or sow right between the eyes. This ensured immediate death, caused little pain, and minimized pen cleanup. Since even four-year-olds work on a farm, my job was to rush the hog into the pen where it was to meet its deadly fate and do the cleanup afterwards. Farmers from near and far came to help butcher the meats and prepare them for the smokehouse. Big Daddy organized the men in carrying out their assignments, and the women assisted Big Mama in boiling the fat for lard and making "lye corn" and soap as well as all kinds of sausage and stews.

"From sun up to sun down" might well describe the length of the average workday on my grandparents' farm, but such a description would have little meaning on this day. Work continued late into the night. Using flickers of flames from the big open pit, glowing embers from underneath the old black wash pot, and reflections from the moon as their only source of light, Big Mama, Big Daddy, and all their friends fervently toiled until the last task was accomplished. As the grownups moved from one undertaking to another, they shared the latest gossip, hummed their favorite tunes, and sang old ballads. The children from surrounding areas—the "Bottom," the "Upper Bend," and the "Lower Bend"— sometimes joined in the singing, but mostly we just lingered around the wash pot waiting for the next batch of cracklings or played our favorite ring games.

That promise my grandfather made to me over and over again many years ago as I straddled his waist with my frail legs and encircled his neck with my tiny arms—that I could return to the farm with him—made it possible for me to enjoy wholesome experiences that I will remember for a lifetime, experiences that I have shared with my children and will share with my grandchildren. The greatest lesson of all to be remembered from Big Daddy's promise is that he always kept his word. I saw something of God in my grandfather. His faithfulness. His dependability. His love. His unfailing promises. God is like that, too. God can be depended on to do just what God says God will do. God always keeps God's word. God always keeps God's promises.

Dear Father, you made the same promise to us that you made to our parents and grandparents before us, that if we but live a godly life and serve you, we will be granted life everlasting. Direct our paths in such a way that we may be fit recipients of your promise. Fill our lives with experiences worthy of sharing with generations to come. Amen.

Thought for the Day: God's promises are true.

Elizabeth Harrison Hicks is vice-president of Kerygma Associates, Inc., a specialized consulting firm in Washington, D.C. She received a B.A. in social sciences from the University of Arkansas at Pine Bluff, and an M.A. in education from the University of Pittsburgh.

Carolyn Holloway

I Gotcha!

"I am with you always, to the end of the age." —Matthew 28:20b (NRSV)

When I was a little girl growing up in Brooklyn, my mother often took me to the community playground. Mom would push me high in the swing—or "swing-swing," as I called it. As I swung high and it felt like I would touch the sky, I must have often had a look of fear on my face, for Mom would say, "It's all right, Carolyn. I gotcha." I would then relax and enjoy the ride. When I climbed too high on the monkey bars, or got scared by the quick motion of the seesaw, Mom would offer her reassuring words, "It's all right, Carolyn. I gotcha." When I rode the carousel at Prospect Park, Mom would strap herself on to the wooden horse and ride with me. I would try time after time to grab the golden ring. I was so scared as the carousel sped up and the world seemed to fly by so fast! But Mom would say, "It's all right, Carolyn, I gotcha." Once Mom said those words, I felt I could do anything. I was confident; all fear was relieved. When it was bedtime, Mom would make me kneel. She taught me how to pray, "Now I lay me down to sleep / I pray the Lord my soul to keep. / If I should die before I wake, / I pray the Lord my soul to take." In essence, it was God's "I gotcha."

Little did I know that my mom was preparing me for some hard times in life: those times I swung too high, times when the carousel of life moved too fast, times that I couldn't get the golden ring. Mom was also preparing me for those times when I would become afraid, nervous, and anxious about situations. At those times, I can hear my mom whisper through the words of God, "It's all right, Carolyn. I gotcha."

As an African American woman in ministry, I experience times when I climb the monkey bars and never reach the top, times when the seesaw seems to stay down but never go up, times when the swing of life pushes me higher than my comfort zone and I have to face the harsh realities of evil on every hand. When I become frightened and want to turn back, God has whispered more than once in my ear, "It's all right, Carolyn, I gotcha. I will be with you always, to the end of the age." When I stand to preach the Word of God and my throat gets dry and my knees begin to shake, when I am expected to prove my calling because of my gender, I hear Jesus say, "Come on, Carolyn. You've got my mind, you've got my strength, you've got my love, you've got my power. My child, I gotcha!"

My sisters, be of good cheer, be ever so faithful, and remember, no matter what happens in your life, God's gotcha!

Thought for the Day: God's got you. He's got the whole world in his hands.

Rev. Carolyn Holloway is the executive minister and minister of outreach at the Mariners' Temple Baptist Church in New York City. A graduate of New York Theological Seminary, she is a member of the federal steering committee for the African Burial Ground in New York, the Black Women in Ministry and Ministers Council of ABC/Metro New York, the New York Coalition of 100 Black Women, and the Baptist Ministers' Conference of Greater New York and Vicinity.

Leatha A. Barrigher Johnson

Look Up and See the Power of God

It seems to me that I've spent half of my life looking down in life: struggles, denials, rejections, and oppressions—and these conditions have caused me to miss seeing the power of God. I, like so many others, have wasted a lot of time looking down at life's struggles and not looking up.

One of my professors told us a story about two Israelites who, having crossed the Red Sea, were looking down at their feet and murmuring. One said, "Look at my feet! They're covered with mud. This is some fine mess that Moses has led us into." As they complained, the mud splattered around their legs. They had crossed the sea all the way to the other side without looking up. The two Israelites anxiously wiped the mud from their feet and garments and never saw the sea parting or the Egyptians swallowed up at God's command. To this day, the two claim that it never happened!

I want to encourage you not to get caught up in denial to handle the dissonance in your life. Look up at life as it is, and seek the wisdom of God. Don't let drugs, alcohol, or TV create an illusion and alienation. The resurrected Christ has won the victory for all, so look up! Keep your eyes on the prize of the high calling of God in Christ Jesus. Remember Psalm 121:1-2: "I will lift up mine eyes unto the hills, from whence cometh my help. My help cometh from the LORD, which made heaven and earth."

We, as African American sisters, have a common purpose in life, and that is to propel one another as we work toward the same goals. We can go further together than we can alone, so let's encourage one another as we seek to stay on track—and keep looking up!

Thought for the Day: "I will lift up mine eyes unto the hills, from whence cometh my help" (Psalm 121:1).

Leatha A. Barrigher Johnson, a licensed Baptist minister, is a graduate of Queens College, LaGuardia Community College, and New York Theological Seminary. She worked with the New York City Family Preservation Program in Bedford Stuyvesant, Brooklyn, New York, ministering to dysfunctional families, before retiring in 1993. She now serves with the new members ministry at the Mariners' Temple Baptist Church in New York City.

Shirley A. Johnson

Accepting God's Will

August 31, 1972, dawned bright and promising. It was the last day of camp, and my daughter, Kym, a camper, and my son, Ricky, a senior counselor, were coming home. Little did I know that before the day was over my faith would be sorely tested.

The sixties and early seventies were heartbreaking years for many parents. The scourge of heroin had swept neighborhoods like a plague. Almost daily I received reports of children who had been students of mine in elementary school who were addicted, selling drugs, or overdosing on drugs. One of my former Cub Scouts had cleaned out his parents' home of everything that could be sold, and my neighbor's daughter was prostituting herself.

Perhaps I was too content. I considered myself

truly blessed, one of God's chosen. Each day I thanked God that I had my health, a teaching position I enjoyed, a devoted husband, and children who made me proud and brought me joy.

My son enjoyed a normal boyhood, adolescence, and young manhood. He attended Sunday school, belonged to the Boy Scouts, graduated from high school, and had completed his freshman year at college.

While some of his peers sold drugs, he delivered newspapers, worked as a lifeguard and counselor at camps, and was a photographer at school. I felt that God really loved me.

On August 31, after seeing his camping units safely on the bus for home, my son and his friend, an assistant counselor, headed for SUNY (the State University of New York) at New Paltz. They never arrived. Both were killed in an automobile collision en route.

I was totally devastated. Previously, I had suffered agonizing personal losses: my sister, brother, mother, and father, in that order. Although bereaved, I had accepted those losses—though not without question, for almost everyone I knew still had their parents and siblings. Perhaps like Job, I was being tested. In time I accepted my losses as God's will.

This time my grief could not be assuaged. I grieved for the promise that would never be fulfilled and the grandchildren I would never have. For over five years I was mired in an abyss of depression from which I could not extricate myself. During this time I was barely able to function or interact with those around me. Since I had always tried to live a good Christian life and keep the Ten Commandments, I could not understand why God had allowed this to happen.

Many years have passed. It has taken time for my anguish to ease, and some pain will always remain. Yet I have a wonderful husband and a beautiful, talented daughter. I count my blessings every day.

God works everything out according to his will, not mine. No matter what God allows to enter into our lives, God knows best and loves us all.

Thought for the Day: In God's own time, everything works out all right.

Shirley A. Johnson, a graduate of Hunter and Lehman colleges in New York, is a retired teacher of the New York City public school system. She now works as a volunteer with Westchester Lighthouse for the Blind in its preschool amblyopia screening program and the "Insights" program for elementary schools.

Emma Jordan-Simpson

Loving Our Daughters

"Beloved, let us love one another; for love is of God; and every one that loveth is born of God, and knoweth God. He that loveth not knoweth not God; for God is love." —1 John 4:7-8

For mothers of African descent, for black women who have perfected the "art of stubborn love," what does "loving" really mean?

What does it mean to love our daughters? So much of what we do to and for our daughters reflects how we value and feel about ourselves. We teach our daughters to be strong, get an education, and be independent; yet we send them subtle messages that they are nothing without a man. Is that how we feel about ourselves? Isn't it impossible to love somebody else when you don't love yourself?

A bright, articulate, young African American woman who was a student at a local college was participating in one of my internship programs. Because of her audaciousness and strong leadership, she was trusted by her peers to organize their closing ceremony. She went off to plan it with the kind of energy I pray for myself, and I was at a loss for words when she returned with tears in her lovely eyes after meeting with a caterer who told her point blank, "Never mind all of that education. You'll never get a man if you don't learn how to cook." Despite such attitudes, I thank the God of Love that she had a mother who truly taught her to reach for the stars—and just not the nearest man.

Loving our daughters must first mean loving ourselves—because we will teach them to feel about themselves whatever we feel about ourselves. If we feel that we are unworthy, our daughters will feel that they are, too. If we feel we are unlovable, our daughters will feel they are, too. If we feel we deserve to be beaten and kicked by someone who professes to love us, well, our daughters will learn to feel the same way.

Loving our daughters means raising our sons.

It has often been said that we teach our daughters to be responsible, giving them chores and responsibilities at an early age, yet we "mushy love" our sons—we give them fewer chores and responsibilities and have fewer expectations of them. How often do we say or hear, "He's a boy! What do you expect?" Yet, what we end up with are daughters who, when ready to make a choice for a life mate, must choose from a pool of men who have been "mushy loved" and not raised.

I was rocking my son to sleep one afternoon, enjoying our intimacy and stolen time together and thinking that this would be the last child of my own that I would get to rock to sleep, I said to him, "Baby, don't ever grow up." But then I started to think—and I quickly changed my mind and said, "No, baby, Mommy wants you to not only get big in your own time; Mommy also wants you to grow up."

Loving our daughters means knowing God for ourselves. God must love God's self because God's relationship with God's children is defined by a love that teaches self-love as well as other-love. Love that is of God encourages growth and models healthy relationships. Yes, love that is of God is stubborn, forgiving, and unconditional— not just when the object of that love is the other but also when the object is the self. This is how our daughters will begin to learn of God's love. Beloved, let us love our daughters as God has loved us.

Thought for the Day: God, strengthen me to be the mother you created me to be. Amen.

Rev. Emma Jordan-Simpson is an ordained minister of the American Baptist Churches in the U.S.A. She is a graduate of Union Theological Seminary in New York City and a member of the Concord Baptist Church of Christ in Brooklyn, New York.

Sybil Adeboyejo Joshua

My Thought Box

I sat in the Dallas airport three weeks ago, awaiting a flight to Corpus Christi to visit my hospitalized husband. I had a two-and-half-hour delay for my connecting flight and lots of time to think about many things. As I sat there praying for my sister, who was to enter the hospital the following week, and pondering over how I should respond to her, the answer dawned on me.

At home I keep a folder labeled "Thoughts." It contains poems, prose, and writings by various people—well known, lesser known, or anonymous. I browse through the folder occasionally and reassess my being in this universe. If I am in a happy mood, my energies and positive outlook are reinforced. If I am feeling a bit down, some of the readings help to pick me up and encourage me to profess that all is well or will be well in

God's time and that all I have to do is trust in God's love and concern for me. When things get hectic and problems seem to pile up or crisis follows crisis, it is important for me to take some quiet time, reflect, and know that "this too shall pass." Then I can concentrate on resolving the problems as best I can or on being a positive support for family and friends.

So I'd like to share with you a prayer from my collection of "Thoughts":

A Lakota Prayer

My spirit is one with You,
Great Spirit.
You strengthen me day and
night to share my very best
with my brothers and sisters.
You, whom my people see in
all of creation and in all
people, show Your Love for us.
Help me to know, like the
soaring eagle, the heights
of knowledge.
From the Four Directions, fill
me with the four virtues of
Fortitude, Generosity,
Respect and Wisdom;

so that I will help my people
walk in the path of
Understanding and Peace.
Amen.

(Used by permission of St. Joseph's Indian School,
Chamberlain, South Dakota.)

**Thought for the Day: Be still and know
that God is God.**

Chief Sybil Adeboyejo Joshua, a lifelong New
Yorker, worked as an administrator with the New York
State Department of Labor many years. The annual
award for outstanding affirmative action activities by a
Labor Department employee has been named the Sybil
A. Joshua Award in recognition of her efforts to assure
nondiscriminatory treatment of staff and clientele. She
is also a recipient of the New York State Brotherhood
Award and a member of the New York Coalition of 100
Black Women.

Darnita R. Killian

Honoring Our Elders

In our youth, we learned a lot from hanging out with our elders. We learned how to cook and sew. We understood strength from listening to their spiritual journeys.

Remember the cold remedies, or being roused from bed on a Saturday morning for spring cleaning? And the times the neighbor across the street reprimanded you—and you knew her directives to stop misbehaving had almost as much weight as your own parents'? Or sitting out in the backyard with Grandpa and having him tell you the world doesn't owe you a thing and a job worth doing is worth doing well? And Aunt Mae telling you that although we came from slavery, no one can enslave your mind, so reach for the stars— at which point she would start humming a familiar Negro spiritual.

Our elders are our teachers. They taught us

common sense, how to treat people. They taught us lessons in faith. They pushed us to excel. Remember our elders. We can learn a great deal from "hanging out with the folks."

On this day, remember a special elder in your life. If that person is still alive, take a few minutes to thank him or her for lessons taught. And remember that you too, Lord willing, will one day be an elder and have a responsibility to teach the lessons of life.

Thought for the Day: I thank God for the elders who touched my life. May I be a blessing to those who will follow me.

Darnita R. Killian is an associate vice-president at the University of San Francisco. She earned a B.A. at Spelman College, Atlanta, Georgia, and an M.B.A. at Clark Atlanta University, was an administrative fellow at Harvard's School of Education, and is currently completing her Doctor of Education degree at the University of San Francisco.

Yolanda King

Loving Ourselves

Imagine being able to overhear a group of your friends and family discussing your life. Are they saying how hard you worked, how many hours you spent at the office, how you were always running here and running there, how you were always on the phone or always tired? Or are they saying that you always loved the Lord, always tried to help your fellow man or woman, that you took care of and loved yourself, and that you took the time to really live your life as God meant you to live it?

"Thou shalt love the Lord thy God with all thy heart, and with all thy soul, and with all thy mind . . . and thy neighbor as thyself." These are profoundly challenging words from Matthew 22:37-39 that we strive to follow and realize in our lives. As formidable as it is to truly love the

Lord and love our neighbors, it has always fascinated me that perhaps the most troublesome task is to correctly love oneself. All too often, as we attempt to juggle the responsibilities of family, careers, and other commitments, the nurturing of our own beings is shortchanged. We expend so much energy being all things to all of the people in our lives that we simply have nothing left to give to building a strong relationship with God. As a result, we are unable to properly care for ourselves. When we do find the courage to say no to some of the demands, we undermine what could be time for productive growth and renewal with feelings of guilt for having said no. The irony is that because we are so consumed with the world's problems, so scattered and conflicted, we end up actually diminishing the quality of the love and support that we are seeking to share.

The truth we must find and claim is found in the words of the Scripture. Love God, then love thy neighbor as thyself. It is a balancing act of learning to give and take; setting aside moments to actively embrace and nourish your spirit, mind, and body; and realizing that the time you spend in restoring, rejuvenating, and nurturing will allow you to more fully contribute to those around you.

Love God. Then love thy neighbor as thyself—not before, not after, but *as* thyself. When all is said and done, you will find the power to honestly love yourself and your neighbor only as you genuinely come to love the Lord.

Thought for the Day: Today I recognize that I am important to God. I will take time for myself.

Yolanda King, the eldest child of Dr. Martin Luther King, Jr., and Coretta Scott King, has been in the midst of the struggle for human rights all of her life. She received a B.A. with honors in theater and African American studies from Smith College in Northampton, Massachusetts, and a B.F.A. in theater from New York University. In addition to an acting career, she is a member of the board of directors of the Martin Luther King, Jr., Center for Nonviolent Social Change and the founding director of the King Center's Cultural Affairs Program. She serves on the partners council of Habitat for Humanity and is a member of the Women's International League for Peace and Freedom and the Ebenezer Baptist Church in Atlanta, Georgia.

Nina Klyvert-Lawson

Casting Out Fear

It is hard to enter into the "coming of age" moment of life. The dreams you've dreamed are envisioned in your mind's eye, and they are sweet—so sweet you can taste them—and so close you can touch them. And as clear as they are in your mind's eye, in reality they appear so very far away and untouchable. They leave a bittersweet taste in your mouth, and the fear of being burned keeps you from going after them, touching them, and holding on.

At some point in our lives, we are all caught in the whirlpool of the emotion called fear. Fear can set in when we live our lives according to the perception of others, when we try to become what we perceive others would like us to be. The more we accept fear, the more it becomes a leech, attaching itself and sucking life from us. We, in turn, entrench ourselves more deeply in the comfort zone of the familiar. It becomes harder and harder to dig out, to break the vicious cycle that exists within. This terror deep inside wears many disguises—and is a debilitating disease. The fear of not knowing who you are, who you want to become, or whether you can trust the person you are can stop you dead in your tracks.

At some point, we will have a wake-up call. We become tired of this roller coaster of terror, the terror of realizing that our life is based on someone's image of us. We don't want to continue in that image. We want the ride to stop; we want to get off. My belief is that this is God extending his hand to us, asking us to grab it and hold on.

The Twenty-third Psalm has helped me to take God's hand and hold on. I read it in the morning; I read it at night. I recite it at any time, out loud or in a soft whisper. Although the entire psalm can quell my fears, two phrases in particular bring me solace: "The LORD is my shepherd, I shall not want," and "I will fear no evil, for you are with me" (Psalm 23:1,4b, NIV).

With continual effort to acknowledge and accept the God within, fear can be conquered. When we acknowledge God's strength, blessings, and love for us, fear is rejected. We acknowledge the fact that we are children of God, and we entrust ourselves to him. We give thanks that God will bless, guide, direct, and comfort us throughout all our days. With God on our side, we appreciate our individual life journey. We live and define our life by our own image. We accept and celebrate our self-worth. We are no longer fearful. In fact, we fear no evil, for God is with us, his rod and his staff comfort us—and our dreams come true.

I trust in the Lord; all fears disappear.
I trust in the Lord; all doubts are removed.
I trust in the Lord; all dreams do come true.

Thought for the Day: "Perfect love casts out fear" (1 John 4:18, NRSV). I have nothing to be afraid of, for God is with me.

Nina Klyvert-Lawson is the dance program director of Harbor Performing Arts, the artistic director of GESTURES Dance Ensemble, and an adjunct faculty member for the Bergen Community Dance Program. She holds an M.A. in dance education from Columbia University's Teachers College in New York and a B.F.A. in theater education/dance from Emerson College in Boston.

Carolyn Ann Knight

When You Fail

━━━━━━━━━━

Failure. It is a difficult word for most of us to comprehend. It is hard for us to believe that we may someday face the possibility of using the word in the same context as our ministry or our calling. When we set out to answer the call from God, prepare ourselves in seminary, or try our wings in service to the community, no one mentions the fact that failure is a real possibility in ministry. No one tells us that, in the course of our ministerial pilgrimage, there will be things that we want to do, visions that we want to realize, dreams we will have for the church that will elude our professional aspirations. *Failure* is a word that we do not like and do not want to hear.

We live in a success-oriented culture. Early in life we are taught to value success over failure.

Walk through any bookstore and you will see rows and rows of books on how to be a success in this life. Few and far between are the books that tell us what to do when we fail. Winning is everything. The only place to finish is at the top. Being number one is not only everything; it is the only thing. That is why failure is such a devastating experience for most of us. We do not expect it. We do not plan for it. We do not want to know failure up close and personal. The expectation of failure in ministry, as well as life, is foreign to most of us.

When I resigned my position as senior pastor of the Philadelphia Baptist Church of Christ in Harlem, New York, on December 31, 1993, almost a full six years after my pastoral ministry began, it was my first head-on encounter with failure. It was the first time in twenty years of ministry that I had to face the fact that I had not measured up to the world's standard of success. Where did we go wrong? On paper, there was still no hint that the Philadelphia church could not or would not succeed. We had a unique vision of reaching new people with the gospel of Jesus Christ; we had an energetic nucleus of people who were attracted to the vision and to the ministry. For the most part, we had the support of people in the community. Yet all of these factors were not enough to get this ministry off the ground. For two, almost three years, I agonized over the possibility that this church might not survive. Essentially, I had failed. My friends tried as best they knew how to comfort me by assuring me that there were many successes in the Philadelphia church, and there were. But I knew, and the congregation knew, that what we wanted to do and what we had set out to do was not going to happen.

I did not look forward to the days following my departure from the church. I knew that in those days I would have to deal with the reality of my failure. There was enough blame to go around, but playing the blame game would not help the healing process begin. In the loneliness and solitude of my own despair, I had questions that would have to be answered. In those days I would be introduced to a new me, a me I had never known before. To my surprise, I discovered that human failure is an amazing place to experience the perfect love of God. What I was to discover in the weeks and months ahead was that God understands that we are prone to fail. The pages of the Bible, both Old and New Testaments, record the operation of God's divine grace in the face of human failure.

James 3:2 tells us that "all of us make many mistakes" (NRSV). Paul tells us in 1 Corinthians 13:9 that as human beings we are in a state of incomplete perfection that is made complete only by the presence of Jesus Christ. This assures us that God is aware of human potential to fail and is prepared to meet us at the point of our failure and help us move beyond failure to where God wants us to be. God's grace meets us at the point of failure to remind us that measuring ourselves by the world's standards will always make us feel inadequate. In life and in ministry we are called to measure ourselves by God's standards. God wants us to place the achievements of our ministry into divine care and keeping. God will bring about the end results that will be worthy of divine expectations.

Failure. We do not like it. It is painful and unpleasant, but in this life and in ministry, it is also unavoidable. Thanks be to God, who measures our human failures against the backdrop of amazing and sufficient grace and points us past our human stumbling to the place we are supposed to be. If we are willing, failure will introduce us to the love and grace of God in an extraordinary way that will enable us to get up and move on with new joy and power for life and ministry.

Thought for the Day: Our difficulties become God's opportunities.

Rev. Carolyn Ann Knight is a native of Denver, Colorado. A graduate of Bishop College, she received her M. Div. from Union Theological Seminary in New York City and was visiting assistant professor of homiletics at Union in 1990-93. She is currently assistant professor of homiletics at the Interdenominational Theological Center in Atlanta, Georgia.

Lola H. Langley

Acts of Worship

> *"Moreover as for me, God forbid that I should sin against the LORD in ceasing to pray for you."* —*1 Samuel 12:23*

As our modern technological advancements stretch across global communities, women find themselves trying to negotiate both the old and new. Even though societal norms still define us as unattractive (like Leah), beautiful (like Rachel), or childless (like Hannah), no matter how we are referenced in today's world, African American women have not only redefined our position and standards in this complex society; we have also redefined our worship.

New definitions cause me to stop and reflect on my personal spiritual journey with Christ. God has been extraordinarily good. His goodness has been manifest to me through his divine gifts: a loving and devoted husband (now deceased); the comfort of seven children and six grandchildren; and many other blessings too numerous to mention. My eager acceptance of God's blessing is automatic. I have learned to expect these blessings with every breath I take, every step I make.

As I anticipate God's blessings, I desire to become more creative as I express my gratefulness for his graciousness. That sweet, quiet voice deep down inside me has brought me to a new understanding, through prayer and meditation. Worship has become part and parcel of what I do and what I say. Personal experiences have become a bridge that supports me through many acts of praise, study, and good works. In my heart I believe that these three are acts of worship. Through praise, study, and good works we become empowered to do God's will.

Each time I pray an intercessory prayer, a prayer of thanksgiving, a prayer for blessings or for protection, I consider this an act of worship. Every time I commit an act of caregiving, make a telephone reassurance call, negotiate daily acts of living for someone unable to act for herself or himself, I consider this an act of worship. Every time I share my knowledge with eager students, intentionally inquire of a young child how are things at school, or direct a needy person to entitlements, I consider this an act of worship. When we give guidance to those who are floundering, pray for the bereaved, visit the sick, and feed the hungry, these are acts of worship.

Each time I eat health-conscious foods, monitor carefully my physical and mental health, participate spiritually and financially in my church, do something uplifting for someone other than myself, study to discern the Word of God, avoid gossip, and learn how to listen to others, I am worshiping. Praise God!

Thought for the Day: Praise God from whom all blessings flow!

Lola H. Langley, Ph.D., is an active member of Convent Avenue Baptist Church. She is also chairperson of the Harlem Tutorial Project, president/CEO of the Association of African-American Gerontologists, Inc., and an adjunct professor at Audrey Cohen College. She received a B.S. from John Jay College of Criminal Justice, New York, an M.S.W. from Fordham University Graduate School of Social Services; and a Ph.D. in gerontology from Walden University in Minneapolis.

Selma Arlette Langley

A Garden Called Faith

It was July 1993. I was lying in a hospital bed when my doctor informed me that I had multiple sclerosis, the crippling, degenerative disease that affects young people.

I experienced shock, fear, anger, and finally relief upon receipt of this diagnosis. After five years of going from doctor to doctor, trying to find out what was wrong, I now had a label to attach to this strange body I no longer knew to be mine.

As days passed and visitors came and went, I felt a peace, calmness, and strength within myself that I'd never experienced before. I slept peacefully and upon rising was full of love and gratitude. I was overwhelmed by my abundance.

Four months following my discharge from the hospital, my condition worsened. As the days went by, my health deteriorated and so did my "faith." What did I ever do to deserve this kind of punishment? Was it my fault? Was I too young? smart? vibrant? Was I "special" to be cursed this way? As time went on, I was unable to get around without a walker or a wheelchair. After returning to the hospital and later being discharged, I was lying in bed when God revealed himself to me in a way that I had never experienced before. I suddenly remembered being a little girl in church. I started hearing songs that once reverberated in my ears from one Sunday to the next—songs such as "We've Come This Far by Faith." And I vividly saw the Scripture that used to be painted on the wall above the pulpit: "I can do all things through Christ which strengtheneth me" (Philippians 4:13).

I couldn't believe how I was able to recall, from memory, Scriptures and songs I had heard as a child! I repeated these songs and verses over and over to myself until something within me allowed me to feel understood and experience the meaning of each of those phrases. It is with the Spirit of rebirth that I experienced that I humbly share this meditation:

> *O Heavenly Father, architect and creator of this temple in which my spirit is housed, in this quiet moment I have with you, right now,*

I surrender all fears, doubts, and worries about what the future may hold for me. I tried to carry my burdens alone, and I only discovered it was an impossible task. I am asking that you resurrect the seeds of faith that you so wisely planted within the core of my spirit when I was a child.

I have been surprised and amazed to learn that this garden, so poorly attended by me, is still alive! Thank you, my Heavenly Father, for being the garden keeper of my faith. Help me, O Lord, to remember to water this garden with courage, love, and joy. Help me to nourish it daily with a humble surrender of my will so that "thy will be done." In this garden, may the roots be so strong that when life's stormy seas come, it will not be moved, and when the storm is over, my garden will grow beautiful flowers of faith, courage, and love.

I now know that this garden called faith is mine to behold and share with the world. Thank you, Heavenly Father, for this gift.

Thought for the Day: God is!

Selma Arlette Langley received her B.A. from Brooklyn College and will soon receive her master's from Banks Street College. Selma has taught for the New York City Board of Education for eleven years, specializing with children who have learning disabilities.

Cynthia Dianne Hardy Lassiter

Bloom Where You Are Planted

I read a story one day about a little plant that was dissatisfied with where it had been planted. The plant was moved several times before finally being put back in its original spot. This story, entitled "Bloom Where You Are Planted," became the basis for a Women's Day message I delivered many times. But more importantly it became an inspiration to me as I struggled to put my own life in its proper perspective. It also helped me to internalize Romans 8:28: "And we know that all things work together for good to them that love God, to them who are the called according to his purpose."

So often we compare ourselves and our situations with someone else's—and we fail to realize that "the grass is *not* always greener on the other side." As sisters in Christ we have a duty to pass on to our children values that our parents instilled in us. We must help our sons and daughters understand that the "abundant life" is not about obtaining things but about being better people in Jesus Christ.

God has given all of us some talent or ability that should be used to his glory no matter where we are in life. God has placed us at a particular place, at a particular time, for a particular purpose, and, yes, all things do work together for good. Belonging to God does not exempt us from life's daily struggles, however. The pressures that come with having a career, raising a family, and being a supportive wife cause me at times to say, "Lord, why?"

"But Lord!" I have protested, "there are problems on the job and problems at the church; my son is having difficulty in school (being a teenager is not easy); my daughters have grown up much too fast (they don't need me); finances are never enough (especially with two in college); families are being torn apart by divorce, drugs, abuse, and so many other things; my mother can barely see or walk; my father is aging; my father-in-law has Alzheimer's . . . ." And yet the answer boomerangs back to me: Bloom where you are planted, and all things—all things, Lord?—yes, all things work together for good to them that love God, to them who are the called according to his purpose.

Lord, I thank you for my husband, children, parents, sisters and brothers, church family, and friends who love me unconditionally.

Thought for the Day: In every thing give thanks: for this is the will of God in Christ Jesus concerning you (1 Thessalonians 5:18).

Cynthia Dianne Hardy Lassiter earned a B.A. in social sciences from North Carolina Central University and is the administrative assistant for Black Clergy, Inc.

Ann Farrar Lightner

One Day at a Time

I awakened that beautiful Monday morning in May as tired and stressed mentally as I was when I had lain down the previous night. It was only 7 A.M. and my head was still on the pillow, but my mind was racing ahead to today's, tomorrow's, and next week's demands. I sat up on the side of the bed as my mind raced on: The radio station needs five meditations, five prayers, and our church ministry summary in order to highlight Mt. Calvary as the "Church of the Week." I need a sermon for the midweek service and two sermons for Sunday morning. I need to prepare for five workshops for the women's retreat I've been invited to lead next weekend. I haven't completed my hospital visitations. The house is a mess. Graduation is this weekend, and I need to prepare for the two-day trip to Dayton.

I must make a hair appointment. The robe was sent directly to Dayton—and what if it doesn't fit!

I was out of control. I had lost it. I felt warm tears run down my cheeks. Then I began to talk to myself. I can't do this. This is too much for one person. I just can't do it all!

After crying for a while and feeling sorry for myself, I called the radio station to ask for more time to submit the material. By the grace of God, I sat down at the computer and began writing meditations on the theme "Order My Steps in Your Word, Lord." But I was still distraught, and it was not until I was on the expressway driving to the radio station to record the meditations that the Holy Spirit clearly spoke to my heart: "Ann, take one day at a time. Live in this day and do not move into tomorrow until tomorrow comes."

I began to cry all over again. But these were tears of joy and thanksgiving. The Spirit gently reminded me of what I had recently preached from Matthew 6, where Jesus taught his disciples to pray, "Give us this day our daily bread" (v. 11). Jesus warned his disciples, "Take no thought for your life, what ye shall eat, or what ye shall drink; nor yet for your body, what ye shall put on . . . for your heavenly Father knoweth that ye have need of these things. But seek ye first the kingdom of God, and his righteousness; and these things shall be added unto you" (vv. 25, 32-33).

I followed the guidance of the Holy Spirit, and not only were weights lifted and my workload no longer a burden, but I was able to successfully make it through what looked like an impossible month. I took it "one day at a time," and by God's grace and mercy I accomplished all the Lord had given me to do.

From that day forward, I have prayed with new understanding, "Lord, give me this day my daily bread." Not next week's sermons. Not next month's mortgage. Not tomorrow's grocery money. Not next semester's tuition. Not even strength for tomorrow's trials and tribulations. I know that God knows my every need and will supply each according to God's riches in glory. Now I'm living my life one day at a time.

Thought for the Day: Give me this day my daily bread.

Ann Farrar Lightner received her B.A. from Boston University; her M.A. from St. Mary's Seminary, the Ecumenical Institute, Baltimore, Maryland; and her

D.Min. from the United Theological Seminary in Dayton, Ohio. She is now pastor of Mt. Calvary A.M.E. Church in Towson, Maryland, and conducts workshops and retreats for youth and adults throughout the country. She also serves as coordinator of Women in Ministry for the Second Episcopal District of the A.M.E. Church.

Sabrina A. Mangrum

Only Living Water Satisfies

John 4 records a conversation Jesus had with a woman at Jacob's well. This woman had come to the well for water, but it is clear that a deeper need brought her to the well alone in the middle of the day. Jesus identifies her problem as having a spiritual thirst that she has sought to satisfy with physical or fleshly things and offers her living water that will permanently satisfy her thirst. As a matter of fact, he tells her that this living water will be a well springing up into everlasting life. Not fully understanding what Jesus is offering but sure it is something wonderful, she asks for this water. Jesus responds by asking her where her husband is. She says, "I have no husband" (John 4:17). Jesus compliments her for her honesty and says she has had five husbands, not including the man she is currently living with.

Jesus begins to address her problem by pointing out that sin is blocking her from spiritual satisfaction. Before Jesus can offer her living water, she must repent of her sinful lifestyle. Her response is to hide behind her religion and get into a discussion of proper doctrine and creed. But Jesus brings her back to the point that her separation from God is the basis for her inability to relate to God. Worship is in spirit and truth. God is spirit, and you cannot approach God apart from a reborn spirit. This is why Jesus told Nicodemus that he must be born again. This deadened spirit must be brought alive by the Holy Spirit in order to worship or commune with God. Sin is merely the response of someone seeking satisfaction through some other means apart from God. When our spirit communes with and worships God, we will find satisfaction for our thirst and no longer need a sinful lifestyle.

This woman had done like many women do today. She had sought satisfaction through men. This woman had a man problem. This woman had thought the best way to find satisfaction was to find the right man. As little girls, women are taught to fantasize about their wedding day. They dream of "Mr. Right," and much of their self-esteem is all tied up in how men treat them or think about them. I dare say that if I asked many women the basis of most of the mental and physical scars they carry in their lives, they would point to some treatment by or experience with a man or men.

This woman had not only one failed marriage but five failed marriages. It is amazing how many women have been hurt so many times already by men, but they keep going back, hoping to find satisfaction through relationships.

No one takes a failed marriage to heart more than a woman. Why is it that, more often than not, women take responsibility for why the marriage didn't work? Some men seem to be able to project guilt even when they were the ones who clearly chose to violate the covenant. They can walk away from many years of intimacy and pick up another woman like they are changing a pair of clothes. Women, on the other hand, are left with their souls bleeding and wide open. Some women are sexually molested as children and yet for years bear the guilt as if it were their fault.

This woman had been rejected by five men.

She had tried five times to find satisfaction with men. Can you imagine the hurt and guilt she must have been carrying to that well? Jesus may have been the first man she had ever dealt with who cared about her as a person and wasn't trying to use her or take advantage of her.

It is really sad that much of the division, fighting, and competing among women is over men. This woman came to the well alone because she had no friends to go with her. The other women despised her because of her reputation with men. When women stop seeking satisfaction through men and seek it through Jesus Christ, there will be more peace among women. Jesus helped this woman to realize that knowing God and worshiping God is far more fulfilling than having any man.

So don't postpone God's purposes and God's ministry for you by waiting for some man. God wants you to be complete in him right now! When the woman at the well understood true worship, she was filled with such satisfaction and fulfillment that she no longer needed her sinful lifestyle. She discovered that the quenching of her deep spiritual thirst came through a relationship with Jesus Christ, the Living Water.

Thought for the Day: My thirst is quenched; my soul has been revived; and now I live in him!

Rev. Sabrina A. Mangrum, a graduate of the University of Maryland at College Park, was licensed to the gospel ministry in 1985 and formally ordained in 1993. She serves as the assistant pastor of Cornerstone Peaceful Bible Baptist Church in Hyattsville, Maryland, where she shares ministry responsibilities with her husband, Rev. Daniel T. Mangrum.

D. Melody Martin

The Joy of Spending

(Read Matthew 6:31-34.)

Money, like time, can be used only once. When spent, it is gone. So choose you this day what you will finance. Choose joy! When opportunities arise that we consider low-pocketbook priorities but are priceless in terms of the human spirit, I have noticed how often we cry poor and say, "I can't afford it; too many things are coming up at once; it's not good to wade too deep." When we allow these joyful opportunities to pass, joyless ones will surely appear and stand ready to claim the reserves we were reluctant to release.

There was a time when my daughter was in college and I was without a job. One fall day, on my way to the unemployment office, I read her letter bemoaning the fact that I would not be coming down to Fisk's homecoming when this one's and that one's mother would be there. She expressed how much she wished I could be there, too. Suddenly, it hit me: If she were sick or an emergency came up, I would be there. So why not go for the sheer joy of it? I signed for my unemployment check, stopped by the bank, made my airplane reservations, and said, "Nashville, here I come."

When I arrived in the city, I went to the dormitory to deliver the surprise of myself. My daughter was still in class, and I waited in her room and visited with her roommate and her mother. Before long we heard her galloping footsteps! Excited, she related that the dorm attendant told her that her mother had come, to which she replied, "No, you saw my roommate's mother." The attendant said, "I know your mother; she's here." Convinced, my daughter bounded up the steps and down the hall for the happy reunion.

Many years later, recalling my daughter's face and footsteps continues to remind me that whenever possible, I must fund the fun and never hesitate to pay the price to firm up friendships and family. So forget always saving for a storm. Sacrifice to bask in the sun! Money so spent will keep you feeling young when you no longer are, because joyful memories are ageless.

Thought for the Day: Today I will fund my fun. Joy, here I come!

D. Melody Martin, New York native, now resides in San Francisco, California. Melody, who is the mother of one adult daughter, contributor Linda M. Aina, is active in education and works at a community college in the Bay Area.

Westina L. Matthews

Obeying Pain

"*The* LORD *our God we will serve, and his voice will we obey.*" —*Joshua 24:24*

I have been told that illness is our best teacher; to kindness and wisdom, we make promises, but pain, we obey. Living daily with pain, I have become obedient. Living with a pain so deep that I cannot find the bottom upon which to rest my feet, I have no choice but to obey God's whispers to my soul. Living with a pain so intense that, with a sharp intake of breath, my questions have turned from a selfish "Why me? And why now?" to a clear and plaintive "What? What will you have me to do, Lord?"

My pain becomes a great clarifier of all that is important and all that is insignificant. No bargains with God, no hollow promises, no demands for release. *My* pain has become *the* pain. *The* pain has become *thy* pain. Cries of "Oh God!" in the middle of the night have changed to cries of "My God!"

Thy cup is bitter, but oh, so sweet! For in thy pain, I hear his sweet murmurings. In thy pain, I feel his comfort. I am free to serve. I am free to obey.

Thought for the Day: "Trust and obey, for there's no other way / To be happy in Jesus, but to trust and obey" ("When We Walk with the Lord," John H. Sammis).

Westina L. Matthews is the vice-president of philanthropic giving at Merrill Lynch, Inc., in New York City. A former member of the New York City Board of Education, she is a member of the First Presbyterian Church of Brooklyn Heights and a member of the Board of the New York Coalition of 100 Black Women.

Hortense J. Merritt

Faith for the Journey

> *"Intreat me not to leave thee, or to return from following after thee: for whither thou goest, I will go; and where thou lodgest, I will lodge: thy people shall be my people, and thy God my God." —Ruth 1:16*

"Anticipation has always been an important characteristic of God's people," states one writer. In the Old Testament, it was Israel's anticipation of the Promised Land, Canaan. For the New Testament believer, it is the glorious hope of eternal life with Christ, our Savior and Lord.

One of the most beautiful verses in Scripture is Ruth 1:16. The story of Ruth and Naomi is a story of love, devotion, and kindness that transcends self-interest. Ruth, a Moabite woman, married a Hebrew, a native of Bethlehem. After his death, rather than returning to live in Moab among her people, she chose to accompany her mother-in-law, Naomi, back to Bethlehem, as expressed in those immortal words above. With an abiding faith in God, Ruth became the wife of Boaz, a kinsman to her first husband. Through this marriage, Ruth became an ancestor of Jesus Christ (see Luke 3:32).

The history of the African American is the story of a people who were brought to the shores of America as slaves. The story of the slaves is one of courage and a giant step of faith in God.

Two important truths empower us to meet the many challenges of life: First, faith in God's Word teaches the believer to wait on the Lord. Proverbs 3:5-6 says, "Trust in the LORD with all thine heart; and lean not unto thine own understanding. In all thy ways acknowledge him and he shall direct thy paths." These words assure us that God is still in control of the universe and that God's will shall prevail. The recorded experiences of the Israelites' crossing of the Red Sea and the Jordan River are examples of God's miraculous power and blessings that encourage us as we obey God and trust his leading. Second, God promises to guide us on our journey. Our

God is ever faithful to his promise.

As African American women, we, too, are on a journey as pilgrims and aliens in a foreign land. We are on a journey to the Promised Land. With a deep faith in God, we are successfully crossing our Red Seas and the stormy Jordans of sexism, racism, and classism. Women are breaking down the walls of sexism in the job market. In the field of education, women are developing new initiatives and charting new directions as college presidents in institutions of higher learning. They bring new visions in mission and ministry.

Yes, when tides are sometimes high, the waters rough, and the winds of adversity stormy, we are sustained by an abiding faith in God. With God all things are possible. When we have faith in God and believe in his promise, God will bring us safely into the eternal Promised Land at the end of our journey.

Hymn writer Samuel Stennett captures the message beautifully in "On Jordan's Stormy Banks I Stand":

> *On Jordan's stormy banks I stand,*
> *and cast a wishful eye*
> *to Canaan's fair and happy land,*
> *where my possessions lie.*
> *I'm bound for the promised land,*

I'm bound for the promised land,
Oh, who will come and go with me?
I'm bound for the promised land.
Amen.

Thought for the Day: "Faith is the substance of things hoped for" (Hebrews 11:1).

Rev. Dr. Hortense J. Merritt is a retired elementary school principal of the New York City public school system. She is the minister of education at New Jerusalem Baptist Church and the campus minister at York College, the City University of New York.

Gloria E. Miller

Living on the Wall

A few years ago a TV minidrama was broadcast entitled "The Women of Brewster Place." This story centered on seven black women who found themselves living in a community of much suffering and sorrow. The lead character of this drama was Maddie Michael, played by Oprah Winfrey. She began the narration of the story by saying, "Years of sunshine and storms had made the women of Brewster Place a family, and in the darkness they stood together."

Brewster Place was walled off from the main artery of the town and had become a dead-end street. Crime, violence, and pain were the fixtures of Brewster Place. It was at the wall that gang members used and sold drugs, ladies of the night made their connections for the evening, muggers and robbers lay prey for old women with their social-security checks, and rapists took advantage of young girls when they paraded at night down the dimly lit street. It was at the wall that children who were neglected by their parents ate with the rats, cats, and dogs out of the garbage cans. Fear and anxiety, confusion and frustration were the order of the day for those who lived by the wall on Brewster Place. What would they do? What would happen to the wall and, more importantly, what would happen to these women?

When we look at the story of Rahab in Joshua 2:8-15 and Joshua 6:20-25, we can see a striking parallel to Brewster place—and to where many of us African American women are living. Rahab was known as a harlot in the city of Jericho, a city that was run by the Canaanites, a city that was walled in. The light of God's love and power was not present. Rahab's house was "upon the town wall, and she dwelt upon the wall" (Joshua 2:15). Rahab realized that the walls of the city were about to come down, and she and her household would be destroyed in the process.

As African American women, we all have walls in our lives. They may be walls that others have built to block our path, or they may be walls that we have built ourselves. Nevertheless, the walls are there—walls of guilt and shame from our past, walls of disappointments from broken relationships, walls from abusive relationships. There are walls of fear as we face our tomorrows and walls of unforgiveness as we harbor pain and anger in our hearts. Walls of unmet financial needs keep us tossing and turning throughout the nights. We face triple jeopardy when confronted with the walls of racism, sexism, and poverty. The problems of life sometimes wall out the sunlight, block our progress, and keep us from experiencing the presence and power of God's love for us.

For too long we have listened to loud and vulgar voices, rude and tactless voices, crude and inconsiderate voices telling us there's no way over, no way under, no way around the walls in our lives.

But just as Rahab and the women of Brewster Place found out, God will exchange our problems for a promise. Rahab received a promise from the spies that was her deliverance. The world may be laden with problems, but the Word of God is full of promises. Do you have a wall of loneliness that makes you feel isolated and alone? Then claim the promise of God that says, "I am with you always, even to the end of the age" (Matthew 28:20b, NRSV).

Thought for the Day: God will exchange our problems for a promise.

Rev. Gloria E. Miller is an associate minister at the St. Paul Baptist Church in Capital Heights, Maryland, and a student at the Howard Divinity School. She is active in civic and African American women's organizations and serves as national treasurer for the National Political Congress of Black Women.

Rosalyn A. Miller

Self-Image

As most women, I have always been weight conscious. When I reached high school age, I wore size eleven jeans and thought of myself as obese. By the time I entered college, however, I was a very proud size five, standing five-feet six-and-one-half inches tall. Family and friends feared I was anorexic; I ate only low-calorie foods like salads (with lemon juice as the dressing), granola bars, yogurt, and diet sodas. My whole life was centered around my slim exterior. I was more confident in dating and going out with girlfriends. Clothes shopping was like being a five-year-old in Disneyland!

Then came marriage. I got married a few months after graduating from college and moved to Los Angeles, where my new husband was already established. Cooking, home decorating, and pleasing my husband became my whole world; trying out new recipes became a hobby. Needless to say, this hobby laid to rest in the lower level (my hips and buttocks).

I had been married for nearly two years when I realized how unhappy I was. Trying to find peace, I began to make trips to my hometown of Little Rock, Arkansas, whenever I had the money (I often bought beyond my financial constraints). After four years of marriage, I decided that California, that man, and I did not mix. I went home to Mama and quickly found employment with the Arkansas governor's office.

During this time, my weight continued to fluctuate. When I went to the doctor for diet pills, he noticed a swelling in my neck known as goiter, which is a sign of a malfunctioning thyroid. The doctor didn't seem that concerned, however, and gave me the prescription for diet pills. I lost weight and was once again an attractive size seven. The goiter began to concern me, however, so I visited an endocrinologist, who ran some tests and determined that a thyroidectomy was necessary. In spite of the doctor's grim prognosis, I awakened from surgery with the same voice—and was eager to use it!

This procedure changed my outlook on the

past as well as the future. The scar in the center of my neck reminds me daily how blessed I am not only to be alive but also to be able to speak for the Lord and his goodness. Although I am no longer slim and trim, my faith remains intact. I have family and friends who love me; I am a valued employee of the federal government; and I have the Lord in my life!

Thought for the Day: "For God has not given us a spirit of fear, but of power and of love and of a sound mind" (2 Timothy 1:7).

Rosalyn A. Miller, a native Arkansan who earned an Associate of Science degree from the University of Arkansas at Little Rock, was appointed executive assistant for the White House Office of Domestic Policy in January 1993. She is a member of the National Association of Female Executives and resides in Washington, D.C., where she is an active member of the Metropolitan Baptist Church.

Marlene Moss-Klyvert

Slothfulness

Acedia or *accidie* is a term used by some theologians to describe the state of a person who fails to do with his or her life all that he or she could do. Accidie characterizes a person who is slothful or lazy. Thank God I have managed to avoid this label! What has guided me in the opposite direction, away from being a slothful person?

I was raised in a Christian household, where a good percentage of my youthful development was steeped in lessons that could always be traced back to the Bible. That meant there was always a force majeure—a greater force—in them. As anyone who has had any exposure to the Bible knows, it contains passages that condemn slothfulness. Proverbs 13:4 says, "The soul of the sluggard desireth, and hath nothing; but the soul of the diligent shall be made fat," and Proverbs 20:4 adds, "The sluggard will not plow by reason of the cold; therefore shall he beg in harvest, and have nothing." Having been raised Catholic, I'm sure I must have also heard the Latin phrase many times, *"Laborare est orare"* ("to labor is to pray" or "to work is to worship"). Given the above forces that were influencing my character development, how could I not adopt the attitude of Proverbs 16:3: "Commit thy works unto the LORD, and thy thoughts shall be established"?

Perhaps this accounts for the fact that I have always been committed to establishing goals for myself and have diligently worked toward achieving them. I think that, as a result of my firm commitment to avoiding the sin of accidie, I have been able to realize a full, giving, and loving life. I can see the personification of my life in the words of *The Prophet* by Kahlil Gibran (New York: Alfred A. Knopf, 1968) when he states:

> You work that you may keep pace with the earth and the soul of the earth. For to be idle is to become a stranger unto the seasons, and to step out of life's procession, that marches in majesty and proud submission towards the infinite . . . when you work you fulfill a part

of earth's furthest dream, assigned to you when that dream was born, and in keeping with labor you are in truth loving life. . . When you work with love you bind yourself to one another, and to God.

Thought for the Day: "Be not weary in well doing" (2 Thessalonians 3:13).

Marlene Moss-Klyvert is the associate professor of clinical dentistry at the School of Dental and Oral Surgery and the director of Advanced Standing Dental Students at Columbia University, New York City, where she has received numerous awards and published several articles for professional dental journals. She is the codirector of the Office of Minority Affairs/STEP Program and the mother of contributing author Nina Klyvert-Lawson.

Willie Mae Nanton

Channels for God

". . . and let the one who believes in me drink. As the scripture has said, 'Out of the believer's heart shall flow rivers of living water.'" —John 7:38 (NRSV)

We often do not realize how we serve as channels for God, how our lives impact those we love, especially our grandchildren. I grew up around my grandparents, and all during the day I would hear my grandmother praising the Lord. As she went about her chores, I would hear her say, "Lord, I thank you! Thank you, Jesus. Lord, I praise your name." As a child I did not fully understand why she was always talking to the Lord and calling on the name of Jesus. I knew there was something special about her because she read her Bible daily and taught us how to pray at an early age.

My grandmother was not an educated woman; she completed third grade. But she was a self-taught person whose faith was unmovable. Every night my two sisters and I would sit with her and study the Bible by kerosene lamp. She was a woman full of wisdom. She taught us that there was nothing we could not do. Her favorite saying was, "You can do anything as long as you put God in front." Because of her strong faith in God, out of her heart flowed rivers of living water. Because she drank from the fountain of life, she became a channel for God. I took my first drink of that living water as it flowed through her without yet realizing how precious that fountain really is.

I now have two grandsons, Christopher and Brandon. After the older was born, he lived his first three-and-a-half years in my home. Every night we would kneel down by the bed and say our prayers together. Christopher always asked if he could sleep with me. However, I knew that during the night as I turned or awakened, I did as my grandmother did in that I would say, "Thank you, Jesus. Praise your holy name. Blessed be the name of the Lord." One night Christopher went to bed before I did, and later that night he woke me up to say, "Grandma, you didn't pray and say 'thank you Jesus' before you went to sleep." "Yes, I did," I replied, "but you were asleep. Now we can say 'thank you Jesus' together."

Rivers are still flowing from one generation to the next—and oh, the joy that floods my soul! If rivers are to flow, we must allow God to use us as channels. Out of our hearts we ought to praise God and offer prayers of thanksgiving with our grandchildren, teaching them early in life to lean and depend on Jesus. Because of the water my grandmother drank, she became a channel for me. And because the fountain never runs dry, I became a channel for my grandchildren. This flowing river of living water never stops. Flowing is active and continuous. It did not stop with my grandmother; it does not stop with me; and it will not stop with my grandsons. God provides opportunities for all grandparents to become channels of living water, to pass this life-giving water on and on and on.

I believe the relationships between grandmothers and grandchildren give us fertile ground for spiritual nurturing. Grandmothers have a special place in God's redemptive plan.

Thought for the Day: O Lord, please make me a channel of your love—for my children, my children's children, and the generations who will follow.

Rev. Willie Mae Nanton is a graduate of the College of New Rochelle in New Rochelle, New York. She received her Master of Divinity degree from Princeton Theological Seminary in 1990 and was ordained in 1991. Rev. Nanton also has a master's degree in social work from Rutgers University, which she received in 1991. She currently pastors the St. Mary United Methodist Church in Burlington, New Jersey.

Mae F. Parr-Jones

A Christ-Centered Commitment

> *"As for me and my house, we will serve the LORD." —Joshua 24:15*

I met James after a period of mourning and making adjustments as a widow. My daughter was a freshman in college, and I was determined to succeed as a single parent. James was a divorcé with two adult male children. He had recently lost his mother and only brother. He was rebounding from a failed relationship and was separated from his sons.

I know now that God was starting to work in our lives from the day we met. James said that he wanted to marry a Christian woman. At that time, he was not aware of my Christian faith. God continued working, and on June 9, 1990, we were married and our daily struggle began.

James and I are opposite personalities. Although we are successful professionals, I was concerned with the baggage we were carrying from past relationships. He was not the primary wage earner, and he was not a practicing Christian. My God, I thought, am I in for trouble! But we really loved each other and wanted our marriage to work more than anything. I knew that we needed Christ at the center of our life. I prayed to God to work a supernatural healing on James so that he would be born again. James agreed to attend church with me, and one day he found Jesus Christ. God's mercy and grace immediately began to bless our lives.

Today, more than four years later, James and I enjoy a loving relationship with Christ as Lord. James is now an officer in our church, and we both serve on many auxiliaries. We share a Christian life that includes our children. We have centered our married life on serving God and our church and know that we can place our daily struggles at the cross, on which Christ died to set us free. As we increasingly enjoy the security of his love and the freedom it brings, we are able to share these same qualities with each other.

Our faith teaches us that before two people can enjoy an enduring relationship, each must enter into a loving relationship with God through faith in Jesus Christ. Christian marriage is much more than the uniting of two people. It is ultimately a way of life based on a bedrock faith in Christ and service to God.

Thought for the Day: Only what you do for Christ will last.

Mae F. Parr-Jones, formerly a senior benefits analyst with Dow Jones & Company, Inc., resides in Manhattan with her family, where she is a member of Mariners' Temple Baptist Church and a leader of the prayer and praise team, as well as a deacon in training.

Patricia A. Reeberg

Seeing Your Sister's Pain

Peninnah and Hannah are introduced to us as rivals in 1 Samuel 1. The writer of First Samuel allows us to sit at the dinner table with their family and watch Peninnah taunt Hannah. We leave there disliking Peninnah. She is the guilty one; she is the villain. We feel nothing but disdain and anger toward her. When Hannah leaves the dinner table in tears, we run after her. We want to console her, to protect her. She is the victim, the one treated unjustly, even though it was God who closed her womb.

Each person in this story has been cast. Peninnah is the villain. Elkanah is the loving husband. Hannah is the "shero." But is it really this simple? I invite you to take a deeper look into this story.

Peninnah was the second wife of a preacher. Her only value was that she was fertile. Thus she had been reduced to a womb, a baby factory— not even an object of lust or desire, just a machine. She had no feelings *to* be rejected. That's why Rev. Elkanah could sit at the dinner table and, in front of her and their children, pledge his love to Hannah. How many times did Peninnah try to answer her son when he asked, "How come daddy loves her more than you and me, mommy?" How many times did she try not to look at her children, not wanting to see their pain when Hannah received more food than all of them? Peninnah's anger, though misdirected, was justifiable.

And what about Hannah? First Hannah allowed her husband to give her a double portion. She made her husband feel guilty because she could not have children, even though it was God who closed her womb. Hannah did not stop her husband from making proclamations of love to her at the dinner table in front of Peninnah and their children. Instead, she rejected them with tears, as others would have given almost anything to hear an expression of love from Elkanah just once. There was also something God was working on in Hannah's life, for God decided to close her womb. What personality trait was so displeasing to God that God would require its repair before God blessed her?

And what about Rev. Elkanah? He was the faithless priest who did not believe God would reverse the decision concerning his wife. He chose bigamy over prayer and fasting. He chose a quick fix over waiting on the Lord. It was his faithless choice in life that created the hostile climate between Peninnah and Hannah.

Peninnah and Hannah teach us what can happen when we refuse to acknowledge each other's pain. Their story warns us not to allow anyone to stand in the way of sisterhood. What I mourn most regarding these two women is the loss of relationship. They teach us the need to move out of ourselves and try to see how our situation is affecting others—and how destructive misguided anger can be for all parties involved.

Do you know a Peninnah? She is angry, in pain, lashing out at the world, feeling used and unloved, willing to be in a relationship without love and respect. Someone needs to reach out to her.

Do you know a Hannah? She is so wrapped up in her own problems that she can't see how she has hurt others. She does not recognize the pain of her sisters, for she is concerned only about herself. Someone needs to reach out to her.

Thought for the Day: Today I will reach out to a sister.

Rev. Patricia A. Reeberg is an ordained minister of the American Baptist Churches in the U.S.A. who serves as the assistant pastor of the St. Paul Baptist Church in Harlem. She was the first African American female executive director of the Council of Churches of the City of New York.

Jacqueline Blair Rhoden

Recipe for Making a Sixty-Year-Old Woman Happy

Ingredients:
  1 cup of memories
  2 pints of satisfaction
  1 teaspoon of fear
  1 tablespoon of goals
  2 pounds of thanks

Step 1: Recapture a picture of a piano in a parlor, family supper together; Sunday morning prayer, grits, bacon, and biscuits; Sunday school, church service, maybe a pastor's visit and a friend to Sunday dinner.

Step 2: Mix with a lust for love and excitement, a daring attitude, and plenty of mischief; a shared love, marriage, tears of pain and disappointment— what a bowl of treasures; age counted by the number of friends, not the number of years; living takes a lot of growing up.

Step 3: Sprinkle fear over a period of time to bring a desperate desire to stay healthy of body and mind; time to grow old, the mystery of the unknown; the diminishing independence, the wandering mind, the struggle to remember; time to reach out to make amends before life's journey ends.

Step 4: Combine these ingredients with goals reached in a profession, hobby, community, and church life, for it takes years to discover who you are and find that measure of contentment.

Step 5: Finally, add pounds of thanks spread evenly throughout the showers of blessings received. Mix with faith and trust to yield strength and, with forgiveness for those who made you cry, live within the laws of God. Then sit back and witness God's love, which is so beautiful.

This recipe makes a serving for sixty more years of happy living!

Thought for the Day: Simmer in God's love today.

Jacqueline Blair Rhoden is a native of Harlem, New York, and a member of Rendall Memorial Presbyterian Church. Now retired, she worked for many years as a licensed school secretary for the New York City Board of Education.

Jini Kilgore Ross

The Wisdom and Power of God

I had been trying to quit smoking—seriously—for a year. There had been earlier attempts, but they could hardly be called "serious." For a solid year, though, as a new member in our church's weekly Bible study, I had hoped to apply my growing faith to a decade-long addiction. I knew my body couldn't tolerate smoking. I was often short of breath and was easily susceptible to respiratory ailments. Yet I enjoyed the taste and aroma of the cigarette, and I was totally hooked. My habit was so bad that when I didn't have a fresh pack on hand, I would raid wastepaper baskets in my house for cigarette butts just to take a drag or two. I didn't know much in my neophyte faith, but I did know enough to reason that if my habit was stronger than my ability to control it, that wasn't saying much for my faith. The Bible study group was my last resort. If I couldn't gain the strength to stop smoking by filling myself up with God's Word, nothing was going to help.

Then one night I had a "nicotine fit" and stormed out of class. When I reached my car in the parking lot that night in search of a cigarette, I realized that two of my class members had followed me. They were two young men who visited our church from time to time; both were on-fire evangelists. I anxiously told them of my dilemma, and with a sense of urgency that I'll never forget, one of them replied, "It ain't real, sister. It's just a trick of the devil."

That was the first time I began to question the reality of my situation. Sure, my craving was real—as real as a stomachache or a toothache—but the problem itself was not the greater reality. It was just the facade of a deeper, hidden reality: lack of trust in God. Could I trust God for the next nicotine fit?

Another night I had a nightmare in which I was at the edge of the mythological River Styx, which leads to the place of the dead. There stood the ghoulishly green-looking ferryman, Charon, who was waiting to cross me over. I was terrified! I was facing death! I began to holler out. I called, "Jesus! Jesus! Jesus!" I woke up calling on the name of Jesus.

We all have individual needs when it comes to our ability to trust God. At that point in my life, I believed in subconscious and conscious levels of perception. I believed that what happened on the subconscious level was the deeper reality. God knew I believed that, so he allowed me to experience my greatest fear at that time, the threat of death, and his deliverance on both the subconscious and conscious levels. I called to Jesus in my sleep, and I called to him in my awakening. That convinced me that I thoroughly trusted him to save me from the clutches of death. But just as important to me was the absolute peace that settled in my room and in my heart. Jesus had heard me. Jesus had rescued me. Praise the name of Jesus! Hallelujah!

The following week I "happened" to read about a woman who had been delivered from cigarette smoking. Her trial had been so similar to mine I could hardly believe it! Her testimony was strong; God had delivered her. I closed the book and knew I would never smoke again. The resolve came. I knew I trusted Jesus.

That Sunday, as I sat at the back of church, the wind of the Holy Spirit began to flow into me. I was caught up for more than a half hour in what I can only describe as an in-filling, an anointing. It felt like the purest love, the strongest power, the greatest joy, the calmest peace. Afterwards, I just wanted to express love to everyone around me.

I wondered for a while about the meaning of my experience that day—the fourth Sunday in September 1975. For one thing, the "feeling" that I experienced has never left me. When God wants me to feel his presence, he manifests himself to me in that same way, though never as powerfully as during the first in-filling. Two months later I read a verse of Scripture that I received as the explanation for what had happened to me: Galatians 3:2. At that point in my life I was reading *The Living Bible* because it was easier for me to understand. This verse simply said in that paraphrased translation: "Let me ask you this one question: Did you receive the Holy Spirit by trying to keep the Jewish laws? Of course not, for the Holy Spirit came upon you only after you heard about Christ and trusted him to save you."

Hallelujah! My habit had led me to a deeper

level of faith. Added to my belief *about* Jesus was now my assurance of my belief *in* Jesus. I trusted him to save me from the grip of death that night, and I have been growing in that trust, with the aid of the Holy Spirit, ever since. It wasn't nicotine that had me bound. It was doubt. Could I trust God for the next nicotine fit? I learned that I could . . . and for much more. Praise the holy name of Jesus!

Thought for the Day: "Holy Spirit, while on others thou art calling, do not pass me by."

Jini Kilgore Ross, an ordained pastor, holds an M.A. from the University of California and an M.Div. from American Baptist Seminary of the West. In addition to editing *What Makes You So Strong?* (sermons by Jeremiah Wright), she is a contributor to *Those Preachin' Women* (Ella Mitchell, ed.), and *Preach On!* (J. Alfred Smith, ed.)

Kim Martin Sadler

God's Will through Dreams

> *"While he was sitting on the judgment seat, his wife sent word to him. 'Have nothing to do with that innocent man, for today I have suffered a great deal because of a dream about him.'"*
> —*Matthew 27:19 (NRSV)*

The revelation of God's will through dreams has long been a part of the experience of faith. God revealed God's self in a dream to the wife of Pontius Pilate, unnamed in Scripture, but who legend says was a woman of faith named Claudia Procla. God revealed to her the innocence of Jesus in a dream, but her husband failed to respond to her warning.

The anointing of God's Word through dreams has also been a part of our African American culture. I can remember how in my family certain dreams were believed to have special meaning—a meaning that had to be confirmed by consulting my Aunt Kate, who interpreted dreams. It was through dreams that God revealed God's self to me. My decision to give my life to Christ came after I experienced a transforming dream. Likewise, God revealed through dreams that I would first give birth to a daughter and later to a son. Most significantly, the true anointing of the power of God's will in my life came in a series of dreams—dreams that warned me that my health was in danger. Several months after having these dreams, I was diagnosed with breast cancer.

Has God given you a warning upon which you should act? Have you avoided taking care of God's temple, your body, because of a lack of money to pay a physician, the fear of having a mammogram, or the fear of being diagnosed with a serious malady? Whether or not this has been your experience, you need to listen to and act on the warning signs that might affect your health. This year, breast cancer will kill over forty thousand women in the United States. African

American women are increasing in numbers as victims. The presence of God the Creator, Jesus the Son, and the Holy Spirit, the Comforter, can come in various, and often mysterious, ways. As with Pilate's wife, God will reveal God's truth to us in ways that are both conscious and subconscious. We must be open to the presence of God, no matter how God appears and speaks to us.

Thought for the Day: God spoke to Pilate's wife, to Jacob, and to the wise men in dreams. Let us be wise women and listen to the voice of God, however it reveals itself.

Kim Martin Sadler is acquisitions editor for the United Church Press, one of the publishing imprints of the United Church Board for Homeland Ministries of the United Church of Christ.

Cheryl J. Sanders

Worship Is Truthfulness

> *"God is spirit, and those who worship him must worship him in spirit and truth." —John 4:24 (RSV)*

It is in conversation with a woman that Jesus makes his most memorable proclamation on the meaning of worship. In John 4:24 Jesus speaks of worshiping God in spirit and truth.

Worship is truthfulness. It is not intolerance, oppression, or cultural conformity. Jesus says we ought to worship according to the truth, the truth revealed to us by God's Spirit, the truth about ourselves before God. Jesus announces a time when the criterion of truthfulness will bring forth the worshipers whom God seeks and sift out those who are lying and playing games. As believers we need not fear the truth, even when it makes us uncomfortable and uneasy, because without the truth we cannot possibly worship God. Truth is not something we impose on others in an intolerant manner. Rather we must embrace and embody it, so that our testimony becomes a credible witness of the reality of which God we are worshiping.

Worship is truthfulness. It is a human tragedy when worship takes the form of oppression. The humiliation of oppressed people is complete when they are forced to worship their oppressor's gods and are threatened and assaulted whenever they worship their own. Our African American slave forebears were deprived by law and custom of the freedom to worship their own gods with their own languages and drums and dances. Even those who converted to Christianity were not allowed freedom of assembly for religious purposes, in shameful mockery of the principle of religious freedom supposedly valued so highly in this country.

Worship is truthfulness. It is not mere cultural conformity. After the end of slavery, many African Americans exercised the freedom to develop their own churches and denominations, but for many the prophetic edge of Christian faith was lost in the effort to use culturally correct worship as a mode of assimilation into the mainstream of American society. But those who worshiped "white" were subjected to the same racist terrorism and discrimination as those who worshiped "black." Worship ought not be seen as a way to deny our cultural identity, nor should it be held up as a standard of cultural conformity. What a tragedy that we sometimes use worship today to reinforce boundaries, to erect barriers, and to remind God of our racial, sexual, and cultural biases.

The Samaritan woman discovered that worship is truthfulness. She learned about who God is, who we are, and our relationships with others. In fact, the core of her testimony to others was the confession that Jesus had told her the truth about herself, which in turn empowered her to speak the truth about God. Jesus crossed the boundaries and spoke the truth, and that truthfulness came forth as water to a thirsty soul. Let the truth be spoken in our own time, and let our hunger and thirst for righteousness abound and be quenched, as we commit ourselves anew to the work and worship of the God we know. Amen.

Thought for the Day: May the God of truth set you free this day to be who you are, not who someone wants you to be.

Cheryl J. Sanders is associate professor of Christian ethics at the Howard University School of Divinity and serves as associate pastor for leadership development at the Third Street Church of God in Washington, D.C. She is an ordained minister in the Church of God (Anderson, Indiana) and the author of several books and articles dealing with African American women and religion.

Elsie L. Scott

Remember Those Who Have Gone Before

"Think not with thyself that thou shalt escape in the king's house, more than all the Jews. For if thou altogether holdest thy peace at this time, . . . thou and thy father's house shall be destroyed . . ."—Esther 4:13-14

Many of you are in a position where you have power or influence over other people's lives. Your position may be that of a supervisor, shop steward, teacher, director, vice-president, or president. Your position may place you in a situation where you are the only black, the only woman. You may have achieved positions or reached levels at which you can brag about your accomplishments. You may have, in essence, "reached the big house." You must realize, however, that even during slavery, some women were given jobs in the "big house" that elevated them above the women who worked in the fields. Regardless of your position, you did not get where you are by your accomplishments alone. Trailblazers opened the doors ahead of you so that you could have the opportunity to demonstrate your abilities.

With status comes not only power and influence but also obligation. Yes, you have an obligation to use your position to help those who are less fortunate. If you are the only black woman in the boardroom, it is your duty to try to open the door for others and to speak out against improprieties. Yes, we are our sisters' and brothers' keepers.

How many times have you seen an injustice being done to a sister or brother and looked the other way, trying to pretend you did not see or hear anything? Many of us have tried to pretend that the world is color-blind and that racism and sexism do not exist. We are often too quick to believe that the misfortunes of others are due only to factors such as a lack of hard work, lack of focus, or failure to be assertive. You need to take the time to investigate the sister's case;

perhaps she does have a legitimate complaint. If you constantly allow injustices to be done to others, one day the same may happen to you.

This is what Mordecai was trying to tell Esther. Esther thought she had made it when she, a Jewish woman, was chosen by the king to be his queen. Nevertheless, a plan was being made to kill her people. At first she wanted to ignore the problem, making excuses about why she could not help. But Mordecai reminded her that though she was queen, she was still a Jew.

Remember, no matter how high you get, you are still a black woman. To paraphrase Mordecai, "Think not that you can escape injustices more than other blacks or women just because of your position. Keeping quiet will not provide an insurance against racism and sexism."

Thought for the Day: We are our brothers' and sisters' keepers—from the outhouse even to the "big house." Don't forget where we came from.

Elsie L. Scott serves as deputy commissioner of training for the New York City Police Department. She holds a Ph.D. in political science from Atlanta University and is author of several articles and monographs on criminal justice.

Lynda Seward

A Magnificent Obsession

What a time to be a woman! Never before have opportunities seemed so limitless to being all that we can be. Never before have we been so socially, politically, financially, and sexually empowered. Why, even Quaker Oat's fictitious pancake queen, Aunt Jemima, has blossomed from her ragtag mammy cocoon to a slimmer, Ultra-Sheen-permed, baubled, bangled, and beaded professional "Black Betty Crocker."

Yet never before have we been so morally bankrupt, so spiritually void, and so egoistically motivated. As we ride this wave known as the "Age of Obsession," we find we drink too much, eat too much, smoke too much, sleep too much. We are cynical, fearful, critical, pushy, angry, and bitter. We're caught up in compulsive promiscuity, going from one unhealthy relationship to another, sometimes with infatuation turning into fatal attraction. We constantly feel we have to improve on the number and quality of our possessions with endless shopping sprees. Madison Avenue has us so bound that we keep on buying things that promise "that pampered feeling," knowing we really don't need them. Even so, these products somehow make us feel cared for.

Furthermore, there is such a high price tag on maintaining our looks that beauty is no longer only skin deep but rather steeped in investments in French manicures, herbal body wraps, enormous hair weaves, custom blended makeup, collagen and hormonal injections, bust and buttocks implants, chemical abrasions, and a few nips and tucks by the plastic surgeon so that we all look like aging Barbie dolls.

We've completely forgotten that the Bible says not to lean to our own understanding (see Proverbs 3:5). We are so propped up by our distorted perceptions and shaky egos and operate from such a dwarfed sense of self that it's no wonder we are confused and flock to these cult therapies that seem to pop up daily. Waiting on the Lord has become passé, especially when we have such easy access to psychic hotlines, palm and tarot-card readers, astrologers, channelers, and the like. I recently met a woman who added a letter to her legal name so that her numerology would be more favorable. What are we doing? If obsessive behavior is the prevailing attitude, how is it that the most Magnificent Obsession— the One in whom we "live, and move, and have our being" (Acts 17:28), just slipped through the cracks?

Let's face it. A lifestyle of holiness is not easy. It takes a lot of work to delve deep into the dark abyss of our subconscious mind and awaken all of our crippling past pain, and then allow the Lord to come in and heal and fill us with his constant presence. And to keep on bearing the fruit of the Spirit is a lifelong task.

Yet anyone who provides my oxygen, breath, bone and muscle tissue, brain cells, red and white corpuscles, all the neurons, ions, protons that make me tick on a daily basis; who monitors my every emotion, thought process, blood pressure, heart and neurological makeup; who from my birth has known the running count of hair strands on my head (I can't even keep up with how many fall out in daily brushings!); and to top it off who thinks nothing but lovely thoughts about me all day—definitely deserves the trouble of me bending over backwards to do whatever it is this kind of God asks, no matter how long it takes, especially since it is only my best interest God has at heart.

And God's benevolence doesn't just stop there. It so constantly enfolds us that in 1 Corinthians 10:13 (NIV) it's promised that "no temptation has seized you except what is common to [everyone]. And God is faithful; he will not let you be tempted beyond what you can bear. But when you are tempted, he will also provide a way out so that you can stand up under it."

Thought for the Day: What a magnificent God we have!

Lynda Seward is a freelance writer living in Newark, New Jersey. Her chief life interests and commitment at this time are ministering to and empowering children from urban dysfunctional families, as well as offering solace to those afflicted with AIDS.

Martha Simmons

A Woman's Place

Hospitals handed out care today, and a woman was there. She pushed bed pans. She operated, waited, bled, and was refused care. She took a temperature and wondered if there was a balm in Chicago, New York, or back home in Hattieburgh.

Political leaders convened today, and a woman was there. She was pursued by a great cloud of witnesses who were there to remind her of her role in salvation history. In the midst of discussions of budgets and bullets, she wrestled with the overwhelming, she bartered, she was silent, and she was heard. She is a member of the elect.

A household awakened today, and a woman was there. She was in the shelter, the shack, and the suburban split level. She was in the bedroom, the kitchen, the car-become-home. She made love, oatmeal, and her way to work. She's become skilled in balancing and familiar with carrying the weight of it all. Glory, glory, she has learned to lay her burdens down.

Factories started assembly lines today, and a woman was there. She punched in, sweated, was clock-driven. She inhaled fumes, smelled no work security, and felt no gold watch, just weight. She made her contribution before the line moved on and sensed grim triumph.

Lord, thank you for placing us in the right place.

A prison turned its locks today, and a woman was there. She stood guard, paid visits, returned to her cell, and tried not to feel too contaminated. Urgency screamed from a cell block. She pondered God's return and wondered if God would stop by prison cells. She mastered waiting, and clung to her sanity with unheralded heroism.

Prostitution row and crack houses did business today, and a woman was there. She claimed customers, stretched out, and burned out. She pretended, repented, was convicted, and faced truth. She asked if these bones can live again, resolved to do rehab, and prevailed in prayer.

A church opened its doors today, and a woman was there. She preached, hailed Mary, handed out food, and was fooled. She wept over a casket, encountered God, and consecrated her courage.

She rejoiced in things unseen but known.

Lord, thank you for placing us in the right place.

Corporations did business today, and a woman was there. She was at the coffee pot, in the boardroom, and at the front desk. She steamed as the coffee seeped. Her presence looming larger, she pulled open the blinds that allowed her to see equal pay and her own company.

Buses rolled down the streets today, and a woman was there. She waited, boarded, and drove. She leaned somehow right in the middle of a crowd, too self-absorbed for chatter. Decades after Rosa, her feet still hurt. She had a transfer point, stepped down, was stepped on, and stepped up again.

Lord, thank you for placing us in the right place.

Troops landed today, and a woman was there. She hunkered down and wondered if tomorrow it would be Bosnia, Haiti, or another one of the little places with so many unhappy faces. She saw no red glare, but there were bombs bursting in air. She wondered what it meant that our flag was still there.

A nursing home registered a patient today, and a woman was there. She turned others over, tossed and turned, was turned away, turned her face to the wall, and anonymously took her turn as the circle was broken again.

Police and firefighters went out on calls today, and a woman was there. She showed up led by a siren and covered by a shield. She rescued and reserved judgment, saw innocence lost again, and knew that law was impoverished without order. She extinguished a blaze and knew that others would burn because they were soul deep.

Lord, thank you, for our eyes have seen
the glory of the coming,
and we can now see a woman's place.
Ever guide us to that place.
Never let us feel conquered in any place,
disabled in any place,
egotistical in any place,
worried in any place,
or wasteful of time in any place.
We go forth, even on the way there,
ever in the right place,
because you have placed us there.

Thought for the Day: And God created woman, and the woman was there.

Rev. Martha Simmons is an ordained Baptist clergy. She received her Master of Divinity from Emory University and her Juris Doctor from New College School of Law.

Laura B. Sinclair

Love Is a Decision and Requires Action

"Love is patient, love is kind. It does not envy, it does not boast, it is not proud. It is not rude, it is not self-seeking, it is not easily angered, it keeps no record of wrongs. Love does not delight in evil but rejoices with the truth. It always protects, always trusts, always hopes, always perseveres. Love never fails."—1 Corinthians 13:4-8a (NIV)

After thirty-four years, I wondered what made our marriage last—especially today, when statistics show that many marriages don't last that long. I believe marriages last when couples make God and Jesus Christ the center of their marriage and take 1 Corinthians 13:4-8a seriously. This Scripture tells us that love is a decision and requires action.

Love is looking forward to helping your mate achieve his or her goal and achieving goals created together as husband and wife. It's when you decide to put love into action and be positive. It's when you think of your partner's needs and how you might meet those needs. It's when you try to understand each other and create the kind of environment for each other that will help both achieve their best.

Love is listening to each other. Love is always finding ways to build each other up, and never tearing down. Love is not being in competition with but supportive of each other. Love is building a trust that cannot be penetrated by outsiders.

Staying married a long time requires a twenty-four-hours-a-day, seven-days-a-week, twelve-months-a-year commitment to work at making the marriage work. It requires that both partners work on bringing out the best in each other. This is done by kind words and encouragement and help for your partner to be the best that he or she can be.

My husband, Troy, has supported me in all of my activities over the last thirty-four years. He has helped care for our children and has driven me to various activities. I have been supportive of him by encouraging him to make decisions that he was finding difficult and showing him in various ways how much I appreciated his love for me. We have always tried to do special things for each other at times other than anniversaries, birthdays, or holidays. As parents, it was important for us to spend time alone with each other without the interruption of the phone or children. Despite our busy schedules, we still made it a point to "date" each other, even when we were only able to go to the diner for a cup of coffee. Even though our children are now grown, we still "date."

We both make the decision to love each other every day. This is love in action—and is possible because God and Jesus Christ are the center of our lives. Staying married begins with love, and love is a decision and requires action. Decide to love, and let the actions be those of 1 Corinthians 13:4-8a.

Thought for the Day: Love one another.

Rev. Dr. Laura B. Sinclair is the assistant pastor of the Antioch Baptist Church of Corona and the associate executive minister for the Parish Resource Center of American Baptist Churches of Metropolitan New York.

Audrey Smaltz

A Faith That Sustains

🔲🔲🔲🔲🔲🔲

"Wouldn't take nothing for my journey," says the title of one of Maya Angelou's recent books.

"If it wasn't for faith, I wouldn't have a journey," says Audrey Smaltz. It was faith that sustained me when I naively left the security of the corporate world seventeen years ago. During my seven-year tenure as Ebony Fashion Fair coordinator and commentator, I trailblazed a style of commentating that was fresh and unique. I blithely assumed that my industry-wide reputation and connections would serve me well as an independent commentator and fashion entrepreneur. Little did I know that shortly after I left Ebony, the trend in fashion-show delivery would change and commentary would be completely outmoded. Not good news for a professional commentator!

Early on, I discovered that faith isn't something you call on when everything is going well. Faith is what you lean on when your client list can fit on a large postage stamp—and half of them aren't paying! Faith sustains you when people whom you trust know that you're going to go forward, and you know you can't go back. Faith is your comforter when you make mistakes, learn from them, make a few more mistakes, and learn from *them*.

I feel as though I have always walked with God, even in years when I was not a regular churchgoer. And I know for sure that I have God as a next-door neighbor; my terrace wall adjoins the exterior wall of the Fifth Avenue Presbyterian Church. As comforting as it is having the house of the Lord as my neighbor, my greatest comfort comes from knowing that I have God in my presence whether at work or at play, in prayer or in celebration. Hebrews 11:1,6 (NRSV) says it best: "Now faith is the assurance of things hoped for, the conviction of things not seen. . . . And without faith it is impossible to please God, for whoever would approach him must believe that he exists and that he rewards those who seek him."

Looking back on my life's journey, I give

constant thanks and praise for the faith that sustains me in my peaks and valleys, my sunrises and sunsets, my joys and my sorrows.

Thought for the Day: Faith, not fear, for this day and always!

Audrey Smaltz is a member of the Mariners' Temple Baptist Church family in New York City. As owner of the company bearing her name, Audrey Smaltz has for the last fifteen years served the fashion industry as a fashion-show manager, organizer, and coordinator.

Stephannie Solomon

Daily Encouragement

"For thou, LORD, hast made me glad through thy work: I will triumph in the works of thy hands." —Psalm 92:4

"Call unto me, and I will answer thee, and shew thee great and mighty things, which thou knowest not." —Jeremiah 33:3

"But seek ye first the kingdom of God, and his righteousness; and all these things shall he added unto you." —Matthew 6:33

Of the many Scriptures that I hold dear and have learned to apply in my life, these three not only motivate me but strengthen me during tumultuous times. The demands and responsibilities of life often appear overwhelming—disciple,

197

wife, mother, women's discipleship leader, educator, relative, friend, graduate student, neighbor. At one point I felt obligated to so many people simultaneously that I desperately needed to prioritize my responsibilities. In doing so, I sought God through daily prayer, meditation, Scripture reading, and the preached Word of God. Consequently, God extended to me his unmatched wisdom and guidance, teaching me that all issues and circumstances germane to Stephannie must have Christ as the adviser. God has always given me what I needed to be his woman, to discard the extraneous impositions of my life, and to live victoriously in the midst of useful and mandatory tribulations. Whatever was best for me, God provided for me in his time.

It is essential to seek God daily. Each day possesses its own challenges, and my adversary, Satan, has made it clear that he desires to sift me as wheat (Luke 22:31). Without Christ actively involved in my life, I would be consumed and needlessly overworked by the cares of life. As the Lord has guided me along, I cannot help but rejoice in what he does. The Holy Spirit confirms and affirms regularly that I am more than a conqueror. Surviving all my trials and tribulations is due to the grace of Almighty God. In my reflective moments I realize that in more than one experience I could have died, lost my mind instead of my hair, or been incapacitated. Even after receiving Jesus, I have not always lived according to his will for me. But through repentance and confession of my sins, I continually find an undeserved love that greets me every day and pushes me onward in the path of righteousness. My life is not perfect or exempt from concerns, but with Christ working on my behalf, I am greatly encouraged to hang in there and look forward to the outcome.

One of the ways God encourages me is by speaking to me through other sisters who love and serve him. I am blessed to have known so many women whom God has used to share my pain, give biblical instruction, and pray for and with me. I have been compelled by their acts of love and tenderness to bear the burdens of other sisters living inside and outside the will of God. I am glad to be a living witness of God's goodness and faithfulness. No struggle in your life or mine is too difficult for God to bear or work out, for the Lord will perfect that which concerns us (see Psalm 138:8). God will enable us to endure, persevere through, and prevail over any and all of life's daily struggles.

Thought for the Day: Oh give thanks unto the Lord, for the Lord is good!

Stephannie Solomon presently serves in the United Baptist Church, Baltimore, in the women's discipleship ministry as discipleship leader. She has a B.S. in elementary and middle school education from Towson State University and an M.S. from Morgan State University.

Joann Stevens

A Sisterly Celebration

The invitation said, "Let's Take a Break! Ramona cordially invites you to a Sisterly Celebration." For most of the day, some forty women, ranging in age from their late teens to early sixties, shared life stories, good food, and words of wisdom and encouragement. On this warm but balmy summer's day, the weather outside was as pleasant as the environment provided by the women inside—most of whom did not know each other.

As our time drew to a close, someone remarked, "You know tomorrow is Ramona's fiftieth birthday?" So we burst into a robust chorus of "Happy Birthday" and chided our hostess for not letting us know to bring gifts. In the loving spirit so characteristic of her, Ramona assured us that this sisterly fellowship was the gift she cherished.

For through such encounters, she said, she gained strength from those who had already trod the paths lying before her and inspiration from those coming behind.

Several women were moved to testify of the blessings they had received from this sisterly gathering and others like it. The day was nurturing for a new mother who had had feelings of guilt for taking time for herself; inspirational for a budding writer seeking the strength to release her inner voice; affirming for a newcomer to the city who was struggling with loneliness; and invigorating for everyone, as we all had been weighed down by the cares of life and needed a little rest. Joining hands, we bowed our heads and prayed, thanking our loving Father for reminding us how much we needed him and each other.

As women on the move, we often take time to nurture and care for others but neglect ourselves. Sisterly celebrations are soul-nurturing love feasts where two or more gather together to play, pray, and affirm each other in the spirit of Christ's love. Coming together to be renewed, we keep ourselves from coming unglued by the cares of daily life.

Have you talked to a sister today?

Heavenly Father, help me to cast my cares upon you, to take time to pray, and be renewed each day in the healing waters of godly fellowship. Amen.

Thought for the Day: How very good and pleasant it is when sisters live together in unity! (Psalm 133:1, paraphrase, NRSV).

Joann Stevens, a public relations executive in Washington, D.C., has been a catalyst in ecumenical ministry as a writer, teacher, retreat leader, and speaker for more than a decade. She is coauthor of *In Goode Faith*, the autobiography of Philadelphia's first black mayor, W. Wilson Goode (Judson Press, 1992).

Edna "Kitty" Summers

In Sickness and Health

"In sickness and in health" is part of the vow made at the beginning of marriage. That's because illness is one of the tests of a marriage. Although most of us simply glide over it on our wedding day, it is a very important commitment.

Neither spouse marries in order to have the other partner take care of him or her. You plan to be a team, to be one. One day, however, you will feel like you've lost your dignity as you hang your head in a toilet bowl at two in the morning while your spouse stands helpless over you. Any shreds of pretense or decency you had left are now stripped away.

Patience, concern, love, and compassion will create a sense of closeness and unity at times like these—and much worse times. Like the Prodigal Son (see Luke 15:11-32), a spouse may stray away. But keep in mind your marriage vow: "in sickness and in health." Sickness doesn't necessarily have to mean pneumonia, cancer, or a physical illness; it may also mean sickness in gambling, drinking, or even extramarital affairs. What then?

The solution to a long and happy marriage is to pray together and forgive one another (Mark 11:25-26) in order to restore Christian fellowship (2 Corinthians 2:7-10), for a divided house cannot stand (Matthew 12:25).

In you, O God, every family on earth receives its name. Illumine the homes of the earth with the light of your love, granting courage to those who care for sick family members and wisdom to those in fearful times of change. We thank you for the gifts of love we have received from mother, father, spouse, child, and friend. As we have been loved by you and by others, so may we love. Grant us peace through Jesus Christ. Amen.

Thought for the Day: Today I will appreciate the soul mate God has given me. Thank you, Lord!

Edna "Kitty" Summers graduated from Tuskegee Institute in Alabama with a B.S. in home economics and earned a master's in elementary education from the State University of New York in New Paltz, New York. She serves as church leaders' coordinator and a member of the United Methodist Women. She's also an active member of the Xi Omega chapter of Alpha Kappa Alpha Sorority, Inc., where she serves as Hodegos, and a volunteer at the Dorchester County Social Services Department.

Dorothy Watson Tatem

Keepers of Dreams

> *"Now faith is the substance of things hoped for, the evidence of things not seen." —Hebrews 11:1*

When her arms hold the promised life, the mother begins to store up dreams that she hopes will find fulfillment in her baby girl. The visions are as much for herself as for the infant. The mother nurtures the images until they have a life of their own. All that she does for and with her daughter imparts these treasures. The elder sows into the younger dreams that she once held dear. Through her dreams she sees within her female offspring blurs of the shapes of possibilities that she would never have grasped for herself.

As the child grows, the mother probes, prods, nurtures, and always holds fast to dreams that sometimes the daughter is too immature or too reluctant to claim or maintain. Over the years there are times when the two, mother and daughter, do not claim the same visions at the same time, and nightmares surface. The two struggle against one another. The dreams gets scrambled but never dissipate. The elder is the tenacious giver and keeper of the dreams. Her very life finds fulfillment in their birth and nurture.

It is irrelevant whether the dreams come to be or not. What is critical is that the mother teaches by example the necessity of dreaming. Time and experience assist in instructing the younger how to hold fast to dreams. It does not matter that the daughter's dreams may end up being the same, variations of, or different faith-fueled images from those of her mother. It is only important that she is taught to dream and is nurtured in the art of dreaming.

The daughter needs to learn to dream in order to realize her wholeness as a person. She also needs to pass the gift on to the next generation. Perhaps the African American family structures are now weakened in part because too many of our mothers are too young to have learned the value of dreams, the hope and strength in dreams. Thus a generation of children grow up with nightmares of hopelessness.

Finally, when the years weigh upon the elder, the daughter gives the gift of dreams to her mother. Dreams of the continuance of the unfolding of life—dreams of peace, love, joy, and worth. The daughter is now the keeper of dreams. The cycle completes itself. Mothers and daughters together are the keepers of dreams.

Thought for the Day: What dreams did my mother pass on to me? What am I passing on?

Rev. Dorothy Watson Tatem is senior pastor of the Camphor Memorial United Methodist Church in Philadelphia, Pennsylvania. She received her Master of Divinity degree from Union Theological Seminary in New York City. This meditation is a tribute to her mother, Mrs. Dorothy B. Watson.

Delphine L. Vasser-Bates

Filling the Emptiness

Have you ever felt all alone, even in the midst of a room full of people? Have you ever felt emptiness surrounding you so powerfully that you wanted to run and hide? Have you ever felt a void that you just couldn't shake? You have experienced a sudden change, a loss of a friend, child, home, spouse, job. Empty! Family and friends attempt to give you words of encouragement. Empty!

And then with a silent cry you begin to pray, "God, will you please fill this void?" And as the days go by, you can hear the still small voice, "I will never leave you nor forsake you. Go ahead and weep, for weeping may endure for a night, but joy shall come in the morning."

You cry out with the psalmist (Psalm 31:9), "Have mercy upon me, O Lord, for I am in trouble; mine eye is consumed with grief." Then you hear the comforting words of God from Psalm 126:5: "They that sow in tears shall reap in joy." Begin to call upon the name of the Lord.

We praise and thank you, Lord, for your touch, for your presence when things seem hopeless. When we are lonely, you indeed fill the void. Thank you for the Holy Spirit, which surrounds us with your love. Amen.

Thought for the Day: Today, I will be quiet and listen for God's still small voice.

Rev. Delphine L. Vasser-Bates is an ordained elder of an African Methodist Episcopal church in Dallas, Texas. She received her B.A. degree from Emerson College in Boston. After a career in insurance, she now serves as a full-time pastor. She also assists in the office of the Reverend John R. Bryant, Presiding Prelate, 10th Episcopal District of the A.M.E. Church.

Joan L. Wharton

My Prayer to the God Who Sees

> *"Wherefore the well was called Beer-lahairoi [the well of the God who sees me]."* —Genesis 16:14

As I reflect on Hagar and the time when the angel of the Lord said that God would make her son great, I realize that she couldn't help but name that healing well "the God who sees me," for at this well God gave her the strength and courage to raise a great nation.

I, too, have a well that's helping me to raise a great nation, not only for *my* sons but for the sons of my foremothers; the sons of my struggling mothers in Rwanda, Haiti, and Somalia; the sons of my mothers strung out on drugs, suffering with AIDS, locked in prisons cells and my struggling mothers yet unborn.

Mothering your son—as an infant, toddler, preschooler, preadolescent, adolescent, college student, want to be a man, should be a man, please be a man, and now is a man—was and is a high calling.

Help me, Lord, to parent this man, preparing him as your king for his future queen. Father, at times I feel unworthy to parent your sons, but I'm thankful for your grace and mercy. I acknowledge that you are the real parent and I am only the one to whom you have given the responsibility until you come back for them again.

Forgive me, Lord, for the times I loved my son too much or not enough. Forgive me for the times my love may have hurt, harmed, or brought danger to him in any way. I just didn't know. I'm thankful that you are the God who majors in seeing the unseen and the not-so-obvious.

I trust you, Father, to deliver my African American son from the obstacles this world tends to put on him. There are so many strikes against our black sons. When the world messes with their minds, you can keep them in perfect peace. The rites of our African passage tell me that it is crucial for our sons' lives to transcend holistically from one stage to another.

Father, your son will continue to become what I put in him. Please allow me to continue to praise him, encourage him, affirm him, and respect him so that he will always be a praiseworthy man, an encourager, one who will affirm, and one who will respect you and others as well as himself.

Father, the greatest gift I can give my son is a worthy, Christlike example. Help me train him in the way that he should go, knowing that your promise is that he won't depart from it (see Proverbs 22:6). Amen.

Thought for the Day: Our children pass through us but belong to God (a paraphrase from The Prophet by Kahlil Gibran [New York: Alfred A. Knopf, 1968]).

Rev. Dr. Joan L. Wharton has a bachelor's degree from the University of Maryland, a master's from Howard Divinity School, and a doctorate from United Theological Seminary in Dayton, Ohio. She is an elder in the African Methodist Episcopal church and serves as the pastor of Bethel A.M.E. Church in Church Hill, Maryland. She has written articles for the National Council of Churches and a handbook for churches to use in developing an effective youth ministry.

Evelyn M. White

Drawing God Down

I can still see Miss Birdie in the clapboard country church of my childhood, her back to the window in the choir loft, the sun painting a shadowy aura around the folds of her aging body. How I longed to be anywhere else! I felt trapped by the drone of the sermon and the shrill voices of the choir, overcome by the musky smell of Never-Tel deodorant and Evening-in-Paris body powder.

On those Sundays when Rev. Broadus announced that there would be "testifying," however, my yearning to leave vanished in anticipation of Miss Birdie's turn. The ardor with which she confessed her "sins" and proclaimed her love of God in Jesus Christ held me spellbound. Nonetheless, her closing statement alarmed me: "I want you all to pray for me. Don't pray that I might not have no trials and tribulations, but pray I get to heaven when I die!"

Already the harshness of the Great Depression had acquainted me, an eight-year-old, with "trials and tribulations." And I knew that Miss Birdie's life on a hardscrabble tenant farm was little different from my own. Why, then, ask the congregation to disregard her earthly suffering in favor of securing her a heavenly home? Every night I was presenting God with a veritable laundry list of wishes!

The next half-century brought little change. I prayed almost continually for deliverance from the terror of life's most fearsome circumstances—loss, abandonment, separation, illness, death. Though I tried, I could not dismiss Miss Birdie's haunting words as a ritualized confession, nor could I dismiss Miss Birdie as a pie-in-the-sky-when-you-die Christian. I came to believe that intuitively she had grasped the meaning of her existence while forging a relationship with God—though year after year it seemed my feet remained stuck in the "miry clay" of anxiety and faithlessness.

Anguish often accompanies a diagnosis of cancer. My own was exacerbated by the belief that I had failed to unravel the mystery of my life, that my prayers had not, in the words of author Simone Weil, "drawn God down." Despite surgery, radiation, and chemotherapy, death appeared to draw inexorably closer, while spiritual transformation grew ever more elusive.

Then one afternoon I fell into an exhausted sleep. I dreamed that I had paced the top of the world so long that I had worn a hole in it. As I tumbled to earth, I heard a crotchety old man scream, "Stop! Stop! Enough already! Stop this minute!" Bewildered, I picked myself up. He trotted toward me, accompanied by a plain-faced woman. "It's done! It's finished. You're ready to move on!" he declared irritably. "Done with what? Move where?" I yelled after him as he strode away smartly. "What does he mean? Where am I going?" I cried desperately, turning to the plain-faced woman. "What has happened to the days of my life? What happens to our work, hopes, prayers, and dreams?" I wailed. "Oh that," she said warmly, gesturing toward a night sky emblazoned with the fire of a million Milky Ways, "All that is used to seed the stars!"

Thought for the Day: What a good testimony will do! There is a balm in Gilead.

Evelyn M. White graduated from Howard University in 1949, received her Doctor of Law degree from New York University Law School in 1963, and earned an M.Div. from Union Theological Seminary in 1984. Evelyn has taught elementary school and practiced law.

Leah E. White

Just Wait 'til Tomorrow

"Those who wait for the LORD shall renew their strength." —Isaiah 40:31 (NRSV)

Sometime ago, while in an airport waiting to board my flight, I watched a young mother and her two daughters. She was carrying the toddler, while the other, who appeared to be about four, was holding her hand. The young mother was struggling to control her four-year-old, who was screaming at the top of her lungs, "Mommy, I want to ride on the airplane now!" The mother tried to appease her by patting her. Then she picked her up and held her in her arms. But the child still cried out, "Mommy, I want to ride on it!" Frustrated, the young mother put down the toddler and began to address the older child. She said in a firm voice, "Can you wait until Mommy gets our tickets straight?" Suddenly the crying child stopped and said, "Okay, Mommy." The mother replied, with a tone of amazement in her voice, "Can you wait a while? Are you sure?" she asked. The little girl replied, "Yes, Mommy."

How often have we been appeased with "just wait"? I remember how my own mother and father would tell me to just wait until tomorrow and how that always gave me a sense of comfort and reassurance. "Just wait 'til tomorrow" implies that things will get better. It suggests that all hope is not lost. It implies that something new is going to happen. It suggests that our prayers will be answered—if we can just wait until tomorrow.

Many of us have spent most of our lives waiting until tomorrow. We've waited for nights to turn into days. We've waited for our dry places to become rivers. We've waited for doors to open that were shut. We've waited for dreams to become realities. We've waited for careers to blossom and ministries to flourish. For many, opportunity has knocked, mountains have become molehills, God has answered prayers. Unfortunately, everyone has not crossed into the Promised Land. So we must still find words of encouragement, believe on the promises of God, and seek strategies for faith building. We must with passion and conviction say, "Just wait 'til tomorrow," for our day will come—if we can just hold on and keep the faith.

After the mother got her boarding pass, she took her two daughters and boarded the plane. They sat several rows behind me, and I could hear the mother say to her daughter, who was now playing with her sister, "See, since you've been such a patient little girl, Mommy's going to take you on a ride in the big airplane."

We must encourage others to faithfully wait upon the Lord—"just wait 'til tomorrow." Regardless of the disappointments of yesterday or the challenges of today, be encouraged and don't give up. Tomorrow promises to bring a greater blessing if you can "just wait 'til tomorrow." Our greatest blessing is yet to come. Just wait on the Lord.

Thought for the Day: "Wait on the LORD: be of good courage, and he shall strengthen thine heart" (Psalm 27:14).

Leah E. White earned a B.S. degree from Morgan State University, an M.S. from Johns Hopkins University, an M.Th. from Saint Mary's Seminary and University, and a D.Min. from United Theological Seminary. Well known for her ministry to women, Rev. White serves as pastor of the Remnant Baptist Church in Baltimore and the administrator of the New Psalmist Christian School.

Lorraine Jacques White

Freed to Love

Why is it so hard for people to love? We really want to genuinely love others and treat people right . . . but sometimes we just cannot do it.

One day when I was meditating on the Scripture about loving your neighbor as you love yourself, the Holy Spirit revealed something powerful to me. The Holy Spirit said, "Lorraine, every conflict that you have with anyone is really a conflict with yourself." Immediately I began to think of people who really get on my "last nerve." For instance, I know a woman who is always causing strife. She has a negative attitude and does bizarre things to draw attention to herself. I said, "Lord, I know I am not like that lady." The next thought that came to my mind was: "Why do you think a person would do such things to call attention to herself?" I know this person is love-starved and has always felt rejected.

I then thought of myself, for I have also always been a love-starved person and feared rejection. My way of calling attention to myself is to pout and withdraw. My acting-out behavior is different from hers, but the root cause is the same. I then thought about all the people I tend to reject who are love-starved, rejection-fearing people. I could clearly see that when I rejected this sister, I was really rejecting a part of my own personality that I do not like.

Since then I have had plenty of other opportunities to become irritated with others. But now I know to ask the Holy Spirit to reveal my own inner conflict and to heal it so that I may be free to love. This has been the most liberating revelation in my entire life. It really is true: every conflict we have with anyone else is really a conflict with ourselves.

Why is it difficult for people to love? It is difficult for people to love because of their own low self-esteem, and we project on others what we do not like about ourselves.

What is your pathway to freedom? Be willing to take a good look at yourself. Admit your weaknesses. Ask the Holy Spirit to help you love and accept others unconditionally, and in so do-ing, you will be able to love and accept yourself. At the very moment you give love, you also receive love. And remember, we can love and accept others, including God, only when we love and accept ourselves.

Thought for the Day: Know the truth, and the truth shall set you free (see John 6:32).

Lorraine Jacques White is vice-president of Faith Records and has earned national recognition as a Spirit-filled, inspirational speaker. She is also the coordinator of Women 'N Touch Ministries, which attracts over a thousand women each month. Mrs. White is a graduate of Robert Morris College in Atlanta, and hosts a weekly talk show for women.

Ruth Whitney

The Value of Suffering

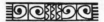

Author Mildred W. Struven once said, "A clay pot sitting in the sun will always be a clay pot. It has to go through the white heat of the furnace to become porcelain."

How we see God affects the way we live our lives. "Someone who knew what he was talking about once remarked that 'pain is the touchstone of all spiritual progress,'" according to Bill W., the co-founder of Alcoholics Anonymous. We can be overwhelmed by suffering if we choose, or we can accept our changing circumstances as enhancing our growth. During painful growth we push our limits and expand our boundaries. If we stay centered on God throughout our painful suffering and let God comfort and quiet us, we won't be traumatized. This does not mean that the pain is not real and that surviving a painful experience won't help us mature spiritually and grow in our compassion for others. Suffering can be valuable in our life, but it doesn't have to consume or control us. With God's help we can keep it in perspective, learn from it, and let it go.

We must suffer with the understanding that life is unfolding exactly as it needs to, for others and ourselves. The way life unfolds is good even when it hurts. And ultimately we can benefit from even the most difficult situations. We do this with the understanding that a Power greater than ourselves is in charge, and all is well. We learn to let go of people we love, people we like, and people we don't particularly care for. We do not allow pain and suffering to sabotage our faith, wreaking havoc with our minds.

As we age, we see more of life and experience more. We have victories along with defeats, moments of great happiness and satisfaction along with moments of rejection and disappointment. With all of this occurring in our lives, we discover a lot about ourselves—including our capacity to love and to accept advice. We gain keener insight into ourselves and others and become well-versed in the harshness, fickleness, and beauty of life.

Keeping a positive spirit is not an easy task because we are constantly challenged. But if we view life's hurdles, such as pain and illness, as stepping-stones, we will be fortified to face the future. We experience pain in growth as we allow ourselves to feel, to drop our protective shield. This is the pain that leads and guides us into better choices for our future.

As I write, I am recovering from an extended illness that could take up to two years to heal. My son has also experienced a lot of pain and at age twenty-seven is on dialysis due to kidney failure related to an incurable disease called lupus. He wrote me these words in a get-well card: Pain is an awful thing. But somehow it is God's favorite tool for getting our full attention. Nothing comes into our lives unless it first passes through the Father's hands, so we must say, as Job did, "Though he slay me, yet will I trust in him" (Job 13:15).

Thought for the Day: Hold on! Our trials come to make us strong.

Ruth Whitney holds a Master of Social Work degree and is a licensed clinical medical technologist. She is a board member of the American Baptist Churches in the U.S.A., chair of the International Ministries Working Group on African Affairs, vice-president to the Brooklyn Area Eastern Baptist Association Ministers' Wives, and educational team member of the International Association of Ministers' Wives and Ministers' Widows.

Tina R. Wynn-Johnson

Faith Can Make a Difference

Much has been made of the image of a step-
parent. As children, we felt little compassion for
Cinderella's wicked stepmother. But the Bible
tells us of Joseph and Jesus, Naomi and Ruth, and
Pharaoh's daughter and Moses—those who
loved another's child as their own and assumed
the responsibility of the child's upbringing.

There is no doubt that entering a stepfamily
relationship, in which new lives and personalities must learn to adjust and respect the other,
places a strain on all involved, but I've learned
in my faith journey that we can do all things
through Christ who strengthens us (see Philippians 4:13). Years ago, when my husband and I
first began to date, he immediately made it clear

that he was a "package deal": "I come with two small children who will always come first in my life. If you can accept that and are to be a part of my life, then you must be a part of theirs."

Little did I know how difficult this task would be. There were strains from the beginning. The children were young (preschool age); their parents were divorcing, and a new woman was in their father's and their lives. The boy was okay—sometimes—but his sister wasn't pleased in the least, and she seized every opportunity to let me know. A few years into this unseemly relationship, and right around the time when I'd decided that all the grief I was getting wasn't worth it, the four of us began attending church together. It was in our new church home that I first heard and still hold dear the words of Hebrews 11:1: "Now faith is the substance of things hoped for, the evidence of things not seen." Somehow, before this experience, I'd forgotten God and faith and prayer and how, if only you believe, God will give you the desires of your heart—and never more than you can bear. It was in this church that I found God again and realized that in fact God had never left me. I learned to pray, trust, and believe. In my new-found faith I realized how much I loved these children and how I wished they could love me.

As with all things in life, time, maturity, and growth heal wounds and take us to the place God intends us to be. In time, God nurtured and blessed each of us. My stepdaughter gave me the honor of being the maiden of honor and my stepson, the best man, as their father and I took our marriage vows one very cold December day. In time, we became a family. Today, my beautiful children are bright, articulate college students and two of the dearest people I know. We have drawn closer to one another and to God. My faith continues to grow ever stronger, and I thank God for these children and for allowing me to be a part of their lives.

Thought for the Day: In due season, we shall reap. Dreams really do come true. Hold on to your faith.

Tina R. Wynn-Johnson, a native of New York state, is the founder of T&T Public Relations, Inc. She is a member of the Mariners' Temple Baptist Church in New York City, where she serves with the media ministry.

Alexis Revis Yeoman

God's Gift of Life

God has given us the precious gift of children to nurture, teach, and protect. Blessing male and female with the gift of life is God's greatest gift to us. Making the decision to have a child is a wondrous thing. It is to decide forever to have your heart go walking around outside of your body. Each time I say grace before a meal, I thank God for the blessing of my son. What a joy it was to feel life inside of me and then to hold that precious gift in my arms! I shall forever be grateful and constantly pray that I may be the mother God would have me to be.

Thought for the Day: Thank you, Lord, for your gift to me.

Alexis Revis Yeoman is the deputy director for public affairs for the Office of National Drug Control at the White House in Washington D.C.

Index of Topics